CAREGIVING WITH CONFIDENCE

TAKE THE *GUESS*WORK OUT OF CAREGIVING!

PAMELA C. REYNOLDS

Caregiving With Confidence: Take the Guesswork out of Caregiving!
by Pamela C. Reynolds

Published by Pamela C. Reynolds

caregivingwithconfidence.com

Edited by Kara Rodriguez and Sherrie Irvin.
Design by Hillary Davis.

ISBN: 979-8-218-06725-0 (print)

The Aging Authority

Dedication

This book is dedicated to my late father-in-law, Gerry "Pappy" Reynolds.

CONTENTS

FORWARD

by Crystel Lynn Smith - Best Selling Author,
Founder of Crystel Clear Business Strategies

I will never forget the day I answered my phone and heard the words no grandchild wants to hear. "Your grandmother was found in her bathtub, we think, about two days AFTER she had fallen." I dropped the phone and immediately rushed to the hospital to be at her side.

My grandmother lived alone, until that day. I knew I had to take her to live with me. What I didn't know was how drastically our lives were about to change. Leaving the hospital that evening, I remember thinking "I wish there was a *HOW TO* book for caring for my grandmother".

A thousand questions ran through my head...

"How do I find the right doctors? How can I keep working AND make sure Grandma is taken care of? Can I find someone I can trust to stay with her through the day? How will I pay for someone to stay with her through the day? How will I get her to and from her doctor's appointments? What medicine is she taking? How do we get them transferred to our pharmacy? What things will I need to make sure she's comfortable in my home? What will we do with all her belongings? What if she falls again? Does she have a medical directive? How can I make my home safe for her?"

We spent the next five years navigating the stormy and choppy waters of elder care. I was certainly not qualified to captain this ship in the middle of this ocean of doctor's appointments, medications, health challenges, physical and occupational therapy, and more! Nor did I have any idea about the expenses or the emotional roller coaster that would be associated with caring for my Grandma.

Four years into our journey my grandmother fell ill and was in the hospital again. This time she had become unconscious and unresponsive. Test after test week after week- no results, no improvement. I was terrified. Finally after a multitude of unreturned phone calls and attempts to talk to anyone who would talk to me about a plan, Grandma's discharge planner recommended she go to a nursing home. My heart sank. I couldn't bear the thought of her being cared for by anyone but me. BUT I knew I was certainly not able to give her what she needed after three weeks of lying in a hospital bed unresponsive without explanation.

So, Grandma was transferred to a nursing home. I walked into the facility that evening after work, physically and emotionally exhausted. I didn't have high hopes or expectations. After all, our hospital didn't offer any solution or improvement for my grandmother. How could I expect a nursing home to be any different?

It *was* different. Pam Reynolds greeted me at the door and introduced herself. She walked me down to my grandmother's room, and inside I was preparing myself to see her in the same unresponsive state I had last seen her in her hospital room.

"Where have you been?" My grandmother almost shouted. I jumped! She was back! Pam explained that they had given my grandmother antibiotics for a urinary tract infection (which the hospital said she tested negative for four times, but that turned out to be incorrect information) and given her physical and occupational therapy that day. It was only day one! I remember thinking that the road to recovery, *and back home*, could be another several weeks. But, if they had done all of this in one day, I knew my Grandmother would be good as new in a matter of weeks!

After allowing me to visit with my grandmother for a bit, Pam came back and spent the next hour calming my ocean of elder-care confusion, teaching me how to gracefully navigate these waters. She was like a breath of fresh air. It was clear that her passion was serving the elderly and their families. We weren't just another room number. My grandmother mattered and so did I. Finally, we had hope.

Since that day, I have continued to benefit personally from Pam's priceless knowledge, compassion, and advice. We remained friends and in the years following and I could always call on her for anything elder-care related (for me, a friend or a client, didn't matter!). Her personal experience in caring for her aging family members, coupled with her extensive experience with the aging population throughout her career makes her a leading authoritative figure in the industry. Her compassion for the aging population, empathy for those who are their caretakers, and passion for serving both have resulted in this extraordinarily heartfelt and essential guide to caregiving. The content in this book will allow you, the caretaker, to understand and prepare for the financial, legal, physical, and emotional responsibilities associated with caring for your loved one.

I can tell you with confidence that a book like Caregiving with Confidence comes along once in a lifetime and is a must have for those caring for aging family members. In it, Pam offers straightforward, detailed, and easy to follow guidance which gives readers the opportunity to reduce and even eliminate the feelings of guilt, strain, and constant lack of time so many of us face as caregivers. Navigating the caregiving world can be a costly and overwhelming challenge. It doesn't have to be. It can, and should be, one of the most rewarding times of our lives! It was for me and my grandmother as a result of Pam's guidance. I am so excited that she has taken the time to put her experience and expertise into this book so that many others will benefit from it as I have. After reading this book and implementing the advice, you will finally be able to get back to enjoying the precious time you were given with your loved ones.

INTRODUCTION

"There are only four kinds of people in the world. Those who have been caregivers, those who are currently caregivers, those who will be caregivers, and those who will need a caregiver."
-Rosalyn Carter

What does it mean to be a "caregiver"? There is no single answer to this question, as caregiving can take many forms. The bottom line is – a caregiver is anyone who supports another person physically, financially, or emotionally. Often the terms "formal" and "informal" are used to describe caregivers. You could say that "formal" caregivers are "professional" and "informal" caregivers are "non-professional". Usually, "formal" caregivers are paid for the services they provide and have certification or training, such as a nurse's aide. "Informal" caregivers provide care to someone, often without payment but usually because of some form of obligation, family or otherwise, to the care recipient. These are not hard and fast rules. Sometimes family caregivers are paid, and you do not have to be blood-related to someone to become their caregiver. These two categories are certainly not definitive. Care recipients also do not fit neatly into explicit categories. One may need to receive care in different forms and durations and during different phases of life. A common thread however is definitive– relying on someone else to provide for your basic needs is an immensely vulnerable and humbling experience, as is caregiving.

Not everyone becomes a caregiver the same way, and no two caregivers are precisely alike. You may not even identify as a caregiver at first. For some it happens abruptly, such as when a family member experiences a debilitating accident or injury and suddenly being a caregiver becomes the most important and daunting role in your life. Or, you may find the role sneaks up on you. It may start with simple routine "check-ins", running errands, and tending to household tasks. After a while, you may find you need to do more and more to ensure they have what they need and are safe. Medical conditions tend to become increasingly complex over time and before you know it, they have become fully dependent on you.

Once I met with a caregiving spouse to complete an assessment for his ailing wife. This man was only in his late 40s. His wife had early-onset Parkinson's disease and her symptoms had progressed dramatically over the course of five years. She wasn't sleeping well, and her anxiety was causing a lot of disruption in their lives. Her medications seemed not to be helping as the doctors had assured them they would. He had reached out to my agency to inquire about what hiring an in-home caregiver could do to help. He was recognizing the need for support as his work was beginning to suffer, and he needed his job but was struggling to balance everything.

In describing the laundry list of things he did for his wife daily, he suddenly stopped and said, "I guess you could say I am a full-time caregiver at this point." I could hear in his voice that he truly was coming to this realization for the first time, even though this had been his reality for five whole years. This is what I refer to as the "slippery slope" of caregiving – when the harsh reality of how all-consuming it can be sneaks up on you. Caregiving becomes increasingly burdensome as things like medication management and doctor's appointments can fill up a calendar quickly, and what was once relatively easy to manage may start to cause interference with your job and other responsibilities.

My introduction to caregiving was during my teenage years. After my grandfather passed away, my grandmother continued to live independently in their home and strongly desired to remain there even though the home and the land it stood upon was more than she could maintain on her own. She was also a good distance away from family and community resources. We lived about 45 minutes from her. I recall the long drives on the weekends to go with my father to mow her lawn and take care of anything else that needed attention around the house that week.

My father was one of her two children, but my uncle had many health issues of his own that led to him predeceasing his mother. My father and my uncle's surviving wife (a registered nurse) were left to do the heavy lifting necessary to support my grandmother. Just like many of the family caregivers I have come into contact with in my career, my father was determined to keep my grandmother in her own home. Together he and my aunt supported her in doing this. I found myself walking alongside my father as he cared for her and watched her reliance on my dad and aunt grow steadily over the course of several years.

It didn't take long for her health to deteriorate. She was soon diagnosed with cancer, followed by the onset of Alzheimer's disease. Rather quickly she needed more and more support to continue living independently. My aunt handled the hands-on care like medication management and bathing, while my dad handled things like bill paying and taking my sister and me with him to do her shopping. They did the best they could to manage her needs at home until it became too much and, ultimately, unsafe for her to remain at home. At that time she was placed in a memory care assisted living community. I vividly remember visiting her there. The community itself was much nicer than I expected, as the vision in my teenage mind of a "nursing home" was quite bleak. Fortunately, my grandmother was lucky to have the retirement funds to pay for higher-end community living. That is not the case for many older Americans. The community was clean, the people working there were friendly. Even so, I thought she had very little quality of life there. Neither did many other residents, who seemed to be struggling with their own physical and mental deficits as they adjusted to an unfamiliar environment. I imagined what it must be like to be trapped inside your body, unable to communicate effectively, and without a familiar face to comfort you.

A few things stuck with me from my experience as my family struggled to manage my grandmother's care needs. First, my dad did his best, but he was constantly under stress and worried about her. Second, he gave his all to make sure my grandmother as well as my sister and I were cared for. I felt for my dad and bore witness to his own self-care faltering in the process. And third, there was no one to provide him with any guidance or reassurance. It was a very lonely and thankless position for him, as it is for many struggling caregivers. I know the decision to place my grandmother in a senior community was hard, and he acted in her best interest. However, I am sure there were times he was riddled with guilt and self-doubt over the decisions he had to make for her as her caregiver.

In the 20th-century, life expectancy more than doubled in all countries in the world[1]. As people live longer and prefer to age in place, adult children find themselves supporting aging family members in increasingly high numbers. According to a study done in 2020, more than 1 in 5 Americans are caregivers, a number that continues to grow as 10,000 people per day turn 65[2]. Another study reported that of all adults with at least one parent age 65 or older, 30 percent say those parents need their support to help to handle their affairs or care for themselves.[3]

Much like parenting, becoming a caregiver for an aging adult is a shock to the system. Your life must change rather drastically to meet someone else's needs. This massive adjustment can be particularly stressful for members of what is referred to as the "Sandwich Generation". Social worker Dorothy Miller coined the term "Sandwich Generation" in the 1980s, predominantly referring to the middle-aged adult caught in the middle of caring for both young children and aging or ailing parents[4]. Caring for someone with an array of needs at any stage of life

[1] Max Roser, Esteban Ortiz-Ospina and Hannah Ritchie (2013) - "Life Expectancy". Published online at OurWorldInData.org. Retrieved from: 'https://ourworldindata.org/life-expectancy' [Online Resource]

[2] NATIONAL ALLIANCE FOR CAREGIVING AND AARP PRESENT: CAREGIVING IN THE U.S. 2020: EXECUTIVE SUMMARY

[3] PEW RESEARCH CENTER REPORT JANUARY 30, 2013 The Sandwich Generation: *Rising Financial Burdens for Middle-Aged Americans* BY KIM PARKER AND EILEEN PATTEN

[4] The 'sandwich' generation: adult children of the aging. Dorothy A. Miller. Social Work Vol. 26, No. 5 (September 1981), pp. 419-423 (5 pages) Published By: Oxford University Press

is undoubtedly challenging. For the Sandwich Generation in particular, they find themselves struggling to meet the needs of all those who depend on them. This balancing act is often managed at the expense of their social life and their own self-care.

The term Sandwich Generation may have been originally intended for adult children who are also parents themselves with their children still living at home, however, it is important to acknowledge that any caregiver can feel "sandwiched" due to an array of varying factors. These individuals may not be parents, but they may also be a spouse, partner, employee, friend, or have other people who rely on them. They may play important roles in their communities. They may have causes they are deeply committed to. Each of these roles require a significant amount of their time and attention, which simply doesn't add up. The highly draining demands on time and energy cause a "sandwiched" person to feel stressed and can cause burnout. You know that feeling of being pulled in multiple different directions, and the guilt that accompanies not being able to give any of them your full attention at any given time? Yeah, that's what sandwich caregiving is!

It is no surprise why many people experience a "midlife crisis" when there is so much to juggle in this phase of life. Many caregivers experience extreme stress, some barely holding it together. There are several risk factors to being a caregiver, including high levels of stress, depression, and even financial hardship. Part of the problem is people thrust into these situations simply don't know what they don't know, and have no idea how to secure and engage the tools and resources they so desperately need.

Being in this Sandwich Generation stage of life myself, I am passionate about supporting this demographic, therefore I am writing this book primarily from that perspective. However, I am confident that caregivers of all kinds can glean something helpful from the information I have to share.

Let me tell you a bit more about my journey in this field. I began my career in senior care shortly after graduating from college with my degree in psychology. My first job was as a social work assistant working with older adults and their families in a residential senior living community similar to the one where my grandmother spent her final years. Driven by my past experience, my goal was to support each resident I had the privilege of caring for as if they were my own family. I wanted to give them the peace of mind that in our care, we were doing everything we could to provide the quality of life they deserved in their final years. Unfortunately, many of my residents did not have family to speak of. I held many hands as they cried, doing my best to fill that gap. As I mentioned, being a care recipient is a very vulnerable position to be in. In senior care, we have the unique privilege of coming alongside people at this difficult stage of life and supporting them. I always wanted the residents I worked with to feel loved, comfortable and respected.

I spent many years working in various roles in senior living but eventually I opened my own home care business. I did this because my observations were that almost every resident I welcomed into my community was there as a last resort. Of course many came to feel right at home in our community, but I knew that remaining at home would have been their preference if they could have made it work. It seemed to me the overwhelming majority of older adults desire to remain living at home. I wanted to offer older adults the ability to do that with loving and professional support. I recalled how my own family struggled to care for my grandmother at home, and what a blessing it would have been to have this kind of support for her at that time.

As I am authoring this book, I am now a certified Aging Life Care Manager, Certified Professional Gerontologist and Certified Dementia Practitioner. I have spent almost twenty years working in the senior care industry. Over the years, I have consulted with hundreds if not thousands of families just like mine but all so very unique in their own ways. I have shared with those families many heartwarming moments and many tears. My past experience with my grandmother is the lens through which I see my work, but with each client encounter, that lens shifts just slightly. It is like being at the optometrist and looking at the rows of letters as the doctor shifts the perspective again and again.

You are likely reading this book because you are a caregiver already or you anticipate it is in your future. However you ended up in this position, it is essential to recognize that even though it may feel like it at times, you are not alone. There are millions of unpaid, informal caregivers in the United States alone. And, almost every caregiver I meet questions themselves if they are doing it right or whether they are doing enough. Caregivers are an extraordinary group of people. Of course, each caregiving journey is as unique as a snowflake, with its own history and relationship dynamics that add further layers of complexity to the caregiving situation. Therefore I urge you not to compare your journey with others, as you are not likely to reap any benefit in doing so. Nevertheless, many universal strategies can be immensely beneficial when implemented correctly and can help keep the family afloat.

As you embark on this journey, you're likely to face new and unfamiliar tasks, and no training manual comes with it. If I could only offer one piece of advice to a caregiver before they really get in deep, it is to gear up and get prepared in advance. The more you arm yourself with knowledge ahead of the crisis, the better off both caregiver and care recipient will be. In the decades I have spent in this industry almost every single client interaction happens in the midst of a crisis, and very little if any preparation has been done. Thus it has become my mission to help people plan in advance to avoid or at least lessen the crises later.

So, let's dive right in! Here are my top five tips for caregivers, to begin your caregiving journey on the right foot.

- **Get organized.** Disorganization is the root cause of an array of problems for caregivers. Help your care recipient get their legal, financial and medical affairs in order now; it will be a huge relief for you later.

- **Understand your care recipient.** Get your arms around the immediate and long term needs of the person you are caring for. As a caregiver, you will frequently be in positions where you must provide information and answer questions. So, get prepared! Being well informed about your care recipient and their needs will better enable you to care for and advocate for them.

- **Educate yourself.** Research and find ways to increase your knowledge on effective caregiving strategies in advance so that you know what you can expect. The more tools and resources you have the better equipped you will be and the easier you can adapt as things change.

· **Set boundaries.** Be realistic about how much of your time and energy you can expend caregiving. Many caregivers have jobs and other people who depend on them. It is vital to set clear limits and communicate them to your care recipient and family members.

· **Seek Support.** Don't tackle this alone! Ask family or friends to take on specific tasks to ease the burden. If you don't have local family support, seek help from churches, caregiver support groups, civic organizations, or senior support services. Look into community resources and services that can help you. Calling the local Area Agency on Aging is an excellent place to start.

You can use the acronym GUESS to help you remember these five tips. I will be revisiting them often and weaving strategies to accomplish each one into the forthcoming chapters. There are five primary areas that need careful attention as you prepare to step into this caregiving role. They are – advocacy, medical, physical, financial and social. Consider the following to help you gauge how prepared you are in each area already:

Advocacy– Are you prepared to step in and speak on your care recipient's behalf when they cannot speak for themselves? Do you have the authority and know-how to do so?

Medical– What are the medical conditions that you will need to assist your care recipient in managing? Do they have chronic conditions that will cause their needs to increase dramatically over time? Are you prepared with alternative plans should they need more care than you can provide?

Environmental– Are the physical living conditions and environment safe and optimal for your care recipient? What accommodations have been or can be made for future needs? What if they cannot continue living where they are?

Social– What social factors affect your care recipient's situation? Is their social network going to be strong enough to provide the support they (and you) will need?

Financial– How will they pay for long-term care services if needed? What are the costs associated with the services they are likely to need in the future?

One of the biggest mistakes a caregiver can make is to only take action when there is a problem. Heed my warning– BE PROACTIVE! In the midst of a crisis it is not the time to begin making plans. When things are stable, it is the time to get your ducks in a row and make sure you have a plan for when things get complicated. The stronger the foundation you build in the beginning, the better enabled you will be to ride out the storms as they come! Nevertheless, if you are already in the midst of a crisis, it is not too late. Take a deep breath and a step back and take control now.

To further assist you with what steps you need to take, I have included checklists and guides related to each chapter's caregiving topic. They are designed to arm you with everything you need along the way. Your diligent preparation will equip you to effectively act as a caregiver and advocate. To start, this chapter includes a self assessment for the five categories outlined above. If any of them are a "weak link" for your care recipient, there are steps you can take now to strengthen it and improve upon the situation. You can surely use this book out of order. Where there is smoke, there is fire. Find the chapter that is most applicable to your current "fire" and start there. Once you have it under control, you can come back and address the other key areas later.

My hope is that this book will provide you with practical guidance as you navigate the complex maze of caregiving. It is my goal to share some of what I consider the most useful insight I have learned throughout my personal and professional experiences with caregiving. Reading this book will help you decipher what care options are available, and what makes sense for your situation within realistic expectations. As you think through them, keep in mind there is immense value in being prepared for increasing care needs over time. Doing so will result in both caregiver and care recipient experiencing a more positive and fulfilling caregiving journey.

For this text, I will be focusing on the "informal", or unpaid family caregiver of an aging adult. However, you may benefit from reading it even if you are another type of caregiver. As I mentioned in the opening paragraph, people find themselves caregivers in a wide variety of circumstances. Perhaps the most common term I have heard used for the care recipient in this industry is "loved one" and I myself have used this term frequently over the course of my career. However, you may be caring for someone whom you do not love, the relationship may be strained, or it may be a professional caregiving arrangement. Therefore, out of respect for the variety of types of caregiver/care recipient relationships that exist, I will use the less personal term "care recipient" in this book. I will also use the pronoun "they" when referring to the care recipient, to avoid assumptions about gender.

INITIAL CAREGIVER SELF ASSESSMENT

How prepared are you in these five key areas? This assessment will help you identify weak areas and prioritize your planning.

(Give yourself 1 point per "yes" answer)

Advocacy – To advocate you must have both the authority and knowledge necessary to step in and speak on your care recipient's behalf when they cannot speak for themselves.

My care recipient has completed the necessary legal documents appointing an agent for healthcare and financial power of attorney. Yes__ No __

I know where my care recipient's legal documents are stored and/or how to access them. Yes __ No __

I have enough personal information about my care recipient to identify them and verify my position as a caregiver (this means demographic information such as legal name, date of birth, location of birth, and social security number).
Yes __ No __

I have enough information about my care recipient's medical record to make decisions about their care and speak to physicians and care providers on their behalf (this means medical information such as diagnosis, providers, allergies, medications, and blood type). Yes __ No __

I know who my care recipient's trusted advisors are and I have their contact information. Yes __ No__

I feel comfortable that the support team my care recipient has in place will be able to help me when needed. Yes__ No__

I have a clear understanding of my care recipient's end of life wishes.
Yes: __ No: __

Total Score ___ out of 7

Medical - To have the ability to assist your care recipient in managing their medical conditions and care needs over time.

I am confident in my understanding of my care recipient's current medical conditions and how they manage them (in other words, I could explain it to someone else).
Yes: ___ No:__

I have a current list of my care recipient's medications (including the prescribing physician, dosage, route, and frequency and the pharmacy that fills it). Yes: __ No: __

I know who my care recipient's medical providers are and have their contact information. Yes __ No __

I regularly attend my care recipient's doctor's visits, or, if not, they keep me informed and I am confident that the report they give me is accurate and complete.
Yes:__ No: __

I keep track of my care recipient's medical condition (things like blood pressure, weight, symptoms, etc. as applicable). Yes: __ No: __

I am confident in my knowledge of the medical system my care recipient relies on. Yes: __ No: __

I know how to access my care recipient's medical records. Yes:__ No:__

I have a good understanding of my boundaries (what I am and am not comfortable doing) for my care recipient if and when they become incapable of caring for themselves. Yes:__ No:__

Total Score ___ out of 8

Environmental - To ensure the physical living conditions are safe and optimal for your care recipient.

My care recipient's current living situation is safe. Yes: __ No: __

We have made necessary accommodations and I feel confident that my care recipient's current living situation is ideal for their current needs. Yes: __ No: __

My care recipient's living situation can be adjusted to accommodate future needs. Or, if not, I am prepared with alternative plans should they no longer be able to live where they are. Yes:__ No: __

I am familiar and comfortable with the emergency preparedness plan that my care recipient has in place. Yes:__ No:__

I am prepared to enact an alternative arrangement should my care recipient need more care than I can provide. Yes: __ No: __

I am knowledgeable of the options available if my care recipient needs in-home support. Yes:__ No: __

I am knowledgeable of the options available for senior living if my care recipient could no longer live at home. Yes:__ No:__

Total Score ___ out of 7

Social – To have awareness of the social factors which affect your care recipient's situation.

I believe my care recipient's current social/emotional needs are being met. Yes:__ No:__

My care recipient has a strong social network. Yes:__ No: __

My care recipient's social network can provide the support they (and I) need. Yes:__ No: __

If needed, I am knowledgeable about the mental health resources that are available for my care recipient. Yes:__ No:__

My care recipient is still driving and I feel safe with them doing so, or if not, my care recipient has reliable transportation to get to and from appointments and activities of their choosing. Yes:__ No:__

I live within driving distance of my care recipient, or, if not, I am confident in the support system in place where my care recipient lives. Yes:__ No: __

Total Score __ out of 6

Financial – To have a comprehensive understanding of your care recipient's finances as well as the costs and payment options related to long term care and senior care services.

I am confident in my understanding of Medicare and Medicaid and how they work. Yes:__ No:__

I know what Medicare plan and/or supplement policy my care recipient has and what their coverage and benefits include. Yes:__ No:__

I am knowledgeable about the costs associated with the long term care services my care recipient is likely to need in the future. Yes:__ No:__

I know the status of my care recipient's financial situation. Yes:__ No:__

I know where my care recipient's financial resources are held and who to contact about accessing funds when needed. Yes:__ No:__

I feel comfortable that the resources my care recipient has available will be enough to fund their long term care needs. Yes:__ No:__

I am free from the burden of bearing any of the financial costs of my care recipient's care. Yes:__ No:__

Total Score ___ out of 7

TOTAL SCORE: __ out of 35

1-12: Underprepared – take comfort in knowing you are in good company, as this is the most common result. You can't be expected to know what you don't know. Reading this book and completing the associated preparation activities will help you improve your score immensely in a relatively short time!

13-24: Above Average – you are probably well prepared in some areas but unprepared in others. That is ok! If there is a section you scored particularly low on, you can certainly hone in on that area to strengthen it. Let this book serve to help you navigate from moderately to fully prepared in no time!

25-35: Well prepared – you are significantly more prepared than the average caregiver. This probably isn't your first time doing this, or you have been fortunate to have had excellent guidance thus far. You may want to use this book as a refresher if you have not reviewed your plans lately as they tend to get outdated relatively quickly.

NOTES

CHAPTER 1

ADVOCACY

"An ounce of planning is worth a pound of cure."
-Benjamin Franklin

Being a caregiver is synonymous with being an advocate. This can be one of the most challenging aspects of caregiving, which is why I start with it. Let me begin by explaining what I mean by advocate. As I mentioned in the introduction of this book, a caregiver is anyone who supports another person physically, financially, or emotionally, not necessarily simultaneously. However, supporting someone as a caregiver in any of these areas of their life you have a responsibility to advocate for their underlying needs being met. For example, if you are only financially supporting them but become privy to a need they are lacking emotionally, you are responsible for assuring that need is given the attention it deserves. This is being an advocate.

In the 1950s, American psychologist Abraham Maslow introduced his theory of the hierarchy of needs in his book, "Motivation and Personality". This is a credible source used widely in psychology and sociology education.[5] The five needs that he outlines are regarded as the basic building blocks that humans need to survive and thrive in life. They are divided into two groups; the deficiency needs and the growth needs. Deficiency needs are the more basic needs that if unfulfilled, can lead to some dire negative effects on a person's well-being. They include needs in the following categories: physiological (things like food and shelter), safety (literal safety from harm and also a feeling of security), social (love and belonging) and esteem (feeling valued, respected and appreciated). Maslow's "growth needs" are more advanced personal growth and fulfillment needs, which cannot even be considered if the deficiency needs are in fact deficient.

As a caregiver and advocate we are responsible for ensuring that the deficiency needs of our care recipient are met. We do not have to be the direct provider for each and every need. However, we do need to ensure that there are resources available to the care recipient to meet each need, even the ones we might not directly be overseeing in our role or relationship with the care recipient.

Being an advocate is no simple task. You will face many unfamiliar situations and obstacles. For example, the medical community (particularly concerning senior care) is a very complex web. Older adults can have difficulty retaining information, staying organized and making educated healthcare related decisions. This means you will need to help your care recipient stay on top of their medical care and records. In addition, they will likely need assistance with legal, financial and other decisions. You are probably not an expert in all (if any!) of these fields. You will undoubtedly become frustrated and even feel hopeless at times. But take heart, as you will be their voice when they cannot speak for themselves. Without advocacy, many seniors and disabled individuals fall through the cracks. You will be responsible for communicating their wishes, preferences and needs and ensuring that their values and beliefs are honored. Your support

---

[5] Maslow's hierarchy of needs: Uses and criticisms. Mary West on July 28, 2022. Medical News Today.

can make all the difference in your care recipient's aging experience and quality of life. Therefore, start preparing well in advance to empower yourself as their caregiver and advocate. The saying an ounce of planning is worth a pound of cure is so applicable in the world of caregiving. The more you do ahead of time the easier the journey will be.

Remember, getting organized is one of my top five tips for caregivers. One of the predominant ways to be organized before a crisis hits is in relation to legal planning. You will need the proper legal documents to give you the authority to effectively act on your care recipient's behalf. These documents must be done ahead of time, before they become dependent on you.

I once had a client named Vicky. Vicky lived with her granddaughter and grandson-in-law, Shelly and Rob. After Vicky suffered a debilitating stroke, they did not hesitate to take her into their home and had taken excellent care of her over the course of close to a decade. There was no doubt in my mind that Vicky trusted them wholeheartedly. They knew her intimately– not just medically but her personality and her innermost wishes and values. Unfortunately, while she made sure her wishes were known to her family, Vicky had not taken the important step of making any legal documentation. Therefore, Shelly and Rob did not have the legal authority to make financial and care decisions for Vicky, nor the ability to take control of managing her affairs if she was unable to do so herself.

Vicky contracted a severe case of pneumonia that caused her to be hospitalized. Her situation became dire as her infection led to sepsis. After a few days she wound up in the intensive care unit on a ventilator. Shelly and Rob were initially able to direct her care as the physicians recognized their relationship as her primary caregivers. However, when Shelly's uncle Kevin (who was estranged from his mother and the family as a whole) caught wind of the situation he showed up at the hospital and started demanding information and inclusion in the decision making. Since he was her oldest son and legally next of kin, the doctors began to take his input over Shelly and Rob's. Kevin insisted on every possible intervention and medical treatment possible. Shelly told me that she believed her uncle was trying to make up for his lack of participation in her care up until that point, and perhaps he was hopeful that she would recuperate and he would have the opportunity to make amends.

The doctors made several attempts to wean Vicky from the ventilator but each time they tried, she was unable to breathe on her own. Shelly and Rob knew that Vicky would not want to remain dependent on a ventilator for any extended period of time. They grew concerned that even if Vicky did come out of her comatose state that her quality of life would be drastically affected. Unfortunately, the physicians were not willing to listen to Shelly and Rob because Kevin would not back down. Kevin went so far as to restrict their access to visit Vicky because he was worried that they might influence an unsuspecting doctor's action. A social worker got involved and consequently Vicky and Rob were allowed to visit, but it was under inflexible terms with a schedule that Kevin had to agree to. This went on for almost two months until Vicky ultimately suffered a pulmonary embolism and passed away in the hospital. Shelly and Rob were heartbroken that Vicky was unable to die on her own terms, and they were not able to say goodbye to their beloved grandmother when she passed.

As Vicky's situation demonstrates, most of the time, it is not the medical intervention you want that is a concern. It is the medical intervention you don't want. Vicky's son Kevin was putting his needs and wishes above his mother's. It seemed as if he was not ready to give up, hopeful for a deathbed reconciliation with his mother. The medical community is trained to save and preserve lives. Which is a good thing, obviously. They are also afraid of lawsuits. Therefore, medical professionals often err on the side of preserving life even when a return to any good quality of life is unrealistic. They tend to shy away from encouraging family members to "pull the plug". I will expand more on this in the next section, but this is the primary reason why everyone should have the legal documents that outline their medical and care wishes and appoint trusted advocates to see those wishes through to fruition.

When it comes to finances, it is the same thing. I find people are often hesitant to appoint a Financial Power of Attorney because they are concerned about the power being abused and money being stolen from them or misappropriated. These things of course do happen. But, those rare situations are much less likely to occur. What is more likely is that if you do not have them, your caregivers are going to have a hard time accessing your money to use for you when you need it, or disputing a financial issue on your behalf when you are unable to. Empowering someone to handle your financial affairs when you cannot do so yourself will save crucial time, money and headache in tough situations. To provide comfort, there are safeguards you can put in place to lessen the likelihood of things like fraud and financial exploitation.

Powers of attorney are only one part of the puzzle. The next section will provide you a basic overview of the legal considerations for an aging or disabled adult. If your care recipient is able, talk to them about setting these things up now to ensure that you have what you need to avoid the hassles Shelly and Rob had to face in advocating for Vicky.

LEGAL PLANNING

As you already know, I am not an attorney. The information provided in this section is based on my experiences guiding people through the legal and medical systems. Additionally, I spent some time working as a paralegal in the estate and elder law field.

My advice is solely meant to help you recognize some of the legal issues you need to think about, and describe some of the problems I have seen due to the lack of proper planning. Please consult a qualified attorney in your state about your specific situation before taking any action.

POWERS OF ATTORNEY

What legal documents does your care recipient need? The first on the list should be what are widely referred to as Powers of Attorney (POA) documents. POAs allow for the appointment of someone you trust as a surrogate decision maker to advocate for you and manage your affairs on your behalf when you cannot due to incapacity. In other words, when you are unable to speak for yourself. Most states separate Financial and Medical Powers of Attorney, therefore requiring two separate documents. In the documents you have two parties: the principal (the one making the appointment and instructions) and the agent (the one being appointed). For this section I will be using those terms.

The Medical Power of Attorney is the document used to appoint an agent to make medical and care decisions for the principal when they cannot. The types of decisions that the agent will have to make usually involve life-sustaining treatments. Life-sustaining treatments are medical interventions that continue someone's life without resolving the life-threatening condition. In other words, the person would die naturally without the medical intervention. In my earlier example, the ventilator Vicky was on is considered a life-sustaining treatment. Some other examples include dialysis, intubation, tube feedings, artificial hydration, certain surgeries and even certain drugs such as chemotherapy, radiation or antibiotics.

In some states, in addition to a Medical Power of Attorney you will need another document known as a Living Will or an Advance Directive. The name of the document depends on the state. This document outlines the principal's wishes regarding medical care and treatment they want to receive while they are still living but are incapacitated. This could occur if the principal is in a coma or even if they have a cognitive impairment that hinders their ability to make sound decisions. This document gives them the ability to make those decisions in advance, and eases the decision-making burden on their agent and family by providing this written guidance.

A principal can indicate in their Advance Directive that they want to be kept comfortable but do not want life-sustaining treatments to be used. However, if they fail to do so, or their instructions are unclear, the agent will be the one who is asked whether to move forward with a particular intervention. It is also going to be up to the agent when the time comes to make the call whether to continue the treatment when the principal is in this condition and not responding to it or improving. Therefore, it is important that Advance Directives be as clear and concise as possible, and to couple that with an in-depth conversation about what the desired outcomes will be. This is the best strategy to empower the agent and provide them peace of mind when faced with making these decisions.

A very common misconception in this area is regarding Cardiopulmonary Resuscitation (CPR). CPR is not an ongoing life-sustaining treatment, but it is considered a heroic measure to restart someone's life when they have stopped breathing and the heart has stopped functioning. While CPR has a reasonably high success rate for healthy adults, the same cannot be said for frail and elderly people. There can be serious physical damage incurred from the act itself, and older people generally already have underlying health conditions, which means that they are less likely to recover and experience any reasonable quality of life post-cardiac arrest. Unfortunately, I have seen this many times.

Because of the much lower likelihood that CPR will result in a positive outcome when someone is frail or chronically ill, some people also wish to have a Do Not Resuscitate Order (DNR) which indicates their preference to not receive CPR. A DNR is not a legal document but rather a medical order, which must be signed by a physician. An Advance Directive can be used to indicate the preference not to be resuscitated, however, a signed DNR order is necessary for it to be enforceable. It is important to recognize the distinction between the two. An Advance Directive, even one that indicates the preference of not receiving CPR, is not enough to ensure the medical providers will refrain from performing CPR in the event of an emergency.

One of the first times I sat in during a consultation with the attorney as a paralegal, we spoke with a client who told us about his experience related to this very topic. He explained to us that they had done an Advance Directive for his frail, terminally ill father that included a provision that he did not want to receive CPR. At Thanksgiving dinner while 20 family members were gathered enjoying a meal, his father had a severe heart attack. When the paramedics arrived, they asked if he had a DNR. They told them yes and turned the Advance Directive over to the medics. In the absence of a signed DNR order, the medics proceeded to perform CPR and take the father to the hospital by ambulance. The family was astonished and angry. They did not understand why the medics had ignored their father's wishes and performed CPR. Upon arrival at the hospital, they were informed that their father had been fully resuscitated and therefore alive but due to lack of oxygen to the brain he was in a vegetative state. He remained in this state and did not wake up, so this family was asked to decide whether to keep him alive on artificial means of nutrition and hydration or let him pass naturally. This was a traumatic experience for them, made worse because it was one they thought they had planned to avoid. However, unbeknownst to them, they had not done enough. They neglected to take the step of getting his physician to sign a DNR order, and have it ready to present to the medics when they called 911.

Recalling this experience, the client wanted to be entirely sure that he had an Advance Directive and also a DNR for himself. The problem with that strategy was that he was only in his 60s and relatively healthy. And, a DNR cannot be signed ahead of time by a healthy person. Do not Resuscitate orders are meant for terminally ill people. Rules governing DNRs vary state by state, but across the board, the doctor must be reasonably certain that CPR will cause more harm than good if it is performed and that is why they are signing it. This could be because you are unlikely in your condition to recover to a quality of life worth living, or because in your frailty it is likely to do irreparable damage.

If your care recipient has not signed a DNR before they become incapacitated, you or whoever is named the agent can sign one when the appropriate time comes. Signing a DNR order may be one of the toughest decisions you are asked to make as a caregiver and agent. But I am here to tell you it is the compassionate thing to do. Whenever I am working with a caregiver who is struggling with this decision, I remember Kate. Kate was a resident in the nursing home where I worked as a social worker. She was one of my favorite residents—so vibrant, positive, full of life and fun stories to tell. I enjoyed visiting with her regularly. She also had an extremely close and supportive family, which was wonderful. Unfortunately, they were very unrealistic about Kate's condition. Kate lived with chronic heart failure, chronic kidney disease, diabetes and multiple other ailments. She weighed close to 300 pounds and was constantly retaining fluid. She was on oxygen around the clock. Despite being in her 80s with multiple comorbidities, Kate was a "Full Code". Full Code means that the patient has not signed a DNR and wants to receive cardiopulmonary resuscitation in the event of a medical emergency.

There is a term in the medical community used to reference patients who are back and forth to the hospital a lot —"frequent fliers". Kate was a frequent flier. Every time her oxygen saturation level would tank or the highest dose of

Lasix wasn't enough to control her fluid retention, back to the hospital she went. Each time her visits were longer. Frequenting the hospital takes its toll over time, physically, emotionally, and mentally. With each hospitalization, I could see Kate deteriorating and I could hear the strain in her voice when I would check in to see how she was doing. She became depressed. One day I asked Kate why she didn't stop going to the hospital and choose to remain in the facility with comfort measures instead. She replied that she would prefer to do that, but she knew it would break her family's hearts. I suggested that she speak with them about it and ask them to consider her wishes. Unfortunately, she never did that, and Kate spent more and more time in the hospital as her condition worsened. One day I counted and over the course of six months she had spent more time in the hospital than at "home" (the nursing home). Ultimately, Kate passed in the cold, sterile hospital intensive care unit where her family could only visit in limited increments and there was nothing comforting there for Kate. Knowing how Kate passed is difficult for me to think about to this day, and it is one reason I am so passionate about educating older adults and their caregivers on the ramifications of end-of-life decisions. In a later chapter I am going to delve further into hospitalizations and expand on more aspects of advocacy related to navigating the healthcare system in general.

Kate's story demonstrates the necessity for the crucial conversations. Unlike Vicky, who had the conversations with her family but did not empower them with the legal tools necessary to act on them, Kate's family had the legal empowerment without the understanding of what Kate really wanted in her end-of-life journey. Both actions are truly necessary to guard against unwanted outcomes and create the possibility of a quality end-of-life experience. Too many families put off the conversations until it is too late, and the miscommunications and misunderstandings that occur during this stressful time can lead to a world of unresolved hurt for those left behind.

Renee's story demonstrates this issue from another angle. Renee was also a resident in the nursing home where I worked. She was in her late 80s and her daughter Julia was her Power of Attorney. However, she had no Advance Directive or DNR in place. Renee had Alzheimer's type dementia and she was aphasic, meaning that she did not speak verbally. She could no longer read or write. She could communicate some with body language and facial expressions but it took a significant amount of careful time and attention to be able to determine what she was trying to say. Eventually Renee stopped eating. She was losing weight and becoming less and less active. When the staff tried to assist with feeding her she would refuse. At the time I was uneducated in the subject and did not recognize what was happening. I know now that Renee was reaching a stage of her Alzheimer's where she was losing her ability to recognize being hungry and thirsty (I will touch more on the stages of Alzheimer's later).

Julia was Renee's only child and the two were very close. She was extremely distraught over her mother's condition. She did not want to entertain the idea of Hospice care; she wanted to keep her mother alive as long as possible. The subject was discussed in a care plan meeting with the medical staff and administrative team of the facility. She insisted that the doctor do something to help her mother. Renee was there in the meeting but of course could not speak. She held her daughter's hand and looked at the ground the entire time. The doctor suggested placing a feeding tube. Julia decided to move forward with placing the feeding tube. Unfortunately, after the tube was placed it was a nuisance to Renee and she would constantly pull at it. She pulled it out within a few days of the surgery and had to go back into the hospital to have it replaced. This happened several times and she also developed infections around the site of the wound. Renee lived for two more years with the feeding tube and it seemed to be a constant source of annoyance for her.

I do not know if Renee would have wanted to live like this but my concern is that she didn't have a choice. Had she and Julia had the conversations while she was still cognizant enough to do so, would she have asked her to keep her alive with extreme measures? Again, I do not know. All I can tell you is that Renee's body language and the look in her eyes did not seem like someone who was living a quality of life they were satisfied with. This brings me to mention the development of a tool called the Dementia Advance Directive.[6] Caregivers and family members of care recipients with dementia face unique challenges when handling end-of-life care decisions compared to those without a dementia

---

[6] dementia-directive.org

diagnosis. Because of these common challenges, Dr. Barak Gaster of the University of Washington developed this tool in collaboration with several of his colleagues as a part of the advance care planning committee. The tool is not legally binding, but it is designed to serve as a supplemental guide in conjunction with a legal Advance Directive, to give insight into what the patient would want in specific scenarios related to dementia and end of life care. It goes into the specifics of dementia symptoms at each stage and outlines the patient's wishes related to each. Dementia is a complex and frightening illness, and this is a very effective communication tool that helps guide the conversation and decision making on such a heavy topic. You can learn more and download the dementia advance directive on the website.

One final piece of advice on this subject is related to the Health Insurance Portability and Accountability Act (HIPAA),[7] which is a law that is designed to protect your privacy regarding your medical records and information. Doctors and medical institutions are bound by very strict rules regarding what information they can release to whom and under what circumstances. Therefore, your legal documents should clearly include language that you are legally entitled to receive this information and the medical provider releasing it is protected from prosecution under these laws. In some states this is included in the Power of Attorney or Advance Directive, in others it is done in a separate HIPAA release waiver.

When it comes to financial matters we turn to the Financial Power of Attorney (or Durable General Power of Attorney). The word "durable" means that the power remains in effect even if the individual becomes mentally incompetent. This document is mainly focused on the financial side of advocacy, although some do include medical related provisions. For example, it may outline the authority to sign healthcare facility admission documents, or to engage and pay care providers for services.

I have been asked why the Financial Power of Attorney is necessary, when an individual could just add their family member to their bank account. Powers

---

[7] hhs.gov/hipaa/for-individuals/guidance-materials-for-consumers/index.html

of Attorney also address access to more than just bank accounts. It can contain provisions for different powers such as talking to credit card companies and other lenders, transferring money, managing investments, and selling assets. These things may be necessary to maintain the person's household or ensure continuous care can be provided. Furthermore, if someone is added to a bank account as an owner, they not only have access to the money immediately, they also become a legal owner of the money in the account. This means from a tax and estate planning perspective that money is theirs, which may not be the intended outcome.

A common misconception is that Power of Attorney documents are not necessary until the person becomes incompetent to make their own decisions. However, in order to be lawfully binding they must be executed when they do have capacity to make decisions. Your care recipient might be capable of signing his or her name but that does not mean that the signature is legally valid. They must understand what the document says and what implications go along with it. The attorney drafting the documents must be confident that they understand what they are doing and are doing so on their own volition. Once they lack capacity they will not be able to execute the documents, which means you will have a much harder time getting medical and financial institutions to recognize your authority and listen to you.

I once had a family come to tour the memory care facility where I was the Administrator. Their mother was in her 70s, and had recently moved in with them when it became apparent she could no longer live on her own due to safety concerns. She had been doing things like leaving the stove on and water running in her forgetfulness. One afternoon the son went to check in on her and found the car running in the garage. She had started it to go to the grocery store, went back in for her purse and then forgot that she had planned to go shopping. That was the point when they decided to move her in with them. However, the transition did not go smoothly. She did not like living with them, she was resentful about having to move out of her house, and she was very vocal about her displeasure. To complicate matters, her first language was German and she had begun reverting back to German, forgetting how to speak in English. The family did not speak German. The dynamics in the home were becoming too intense to manage, so they had started looking for a facility for her. As we went over the admission paperwork, I discovered that the children did not have a power of attorney for their mother. They explained to me that they had already faced an array of issues because of this, such as in dealing with the sale of her home and other financial affairs. Her bank wouldn't speak to them without her consent, and she wouldn't give it to them in her hostile mentality. Unfortunately, the facility I worked for wouldn't accept her as a resident without legal Guardianship in place. This family was stuck between a rock and a hard place because they were trying to act in her best interest and keep her safe, but she couldn't recognize that, and without her cooperation there wasn't much they could do.

This family had to go to court to fight for that power (Guardianship) which is a lengthy (and expensive) process. Not only that, but going the Guardianship route means the courts not only have to approve your authority, but that you also remain accountable to them ongoing. That means every year you will have to submit documentation regarding the decision you have made, actions you have taken, expenses you have paid and more. Having the proper documents in advance will avoid this arduous task later. So, do not wait until your care recipient is deemed incompetent to meet with a lawyer, do it now.

One of the most challenging aspects of legal planning is deciding who should take on the various roles. Many people default to their spouse, or oldest child. However, this may not make the most sense in every situation. The agent does not even have to be a family member. But, family members are often chosen because the responsibility is weighty. Many people are only comfortable asking a blood relative to bear the responsibility. Family or not, there are a few considerations that are most important when choosing an agent (medical or financial). They should be an individual who knows the principal well and can be trusted to act in the principal's best interest. Furthermore, they should have the demonstrated ability to remain calm under duress. It is also important that the agent be free from financial struggles, legal struggles, emotional and mental health struggles, or any other personal difficulties. Finally, the agent should understand their responsibility and be accepting of it. It is crucial to check with them before naming them as there may be circumstances that make them unable to serve. For example, the ideal agent may have too many commitments and responsibilities already and are therefore stretched too thin to serve effectively.

If your care recipient is uncomfortable with giving this type of authority to an agent while they have capacity, as I mentioned earlier there are protections they can put in place to alleviate their concerns. One option is drafting the documents with a "springing" provision. You may have heard of "springing" powers of attorney – that means, the authority "springs" into effect when the individual becomes incapacitated. Therefore, a physician must first make the determination that the principal is incapable of making an informed decision, then the agent's legal authority to make the decision for them is enacted. Many people like the idea of this provision because it provides protection from unauthorized use of this power. However, it is important to recognize that using a springing provision causes a delay when the need to use it arises. This could cause problems for the agent making decisions or being able to take actions in a timely manner. If you use a springing provision, the document will also need to define the "trigger" for determining incapacity and what the documented requirement will be. For example, can any doctor make this determination? Will more than one doctor's opinion be needed? These gray areas may make it difficult, and you must weigh the pros and cons of putting this kind of protective provision in the documents.

Another tactic your care recipient may find attractive to counteract potential for abuse of power is to limit the scope of the power of the agent. For example, you can state that the agent does not have the power to sign the principal into a nursing facility. Or, they do not have the power to sell your property. Bear in mind however, that limiting powers does make the documents harder to implement when you need them to be used. The narrower the scope, the less likely they will be accepted and the more scrutinized they will be, which can cost precious time in an emergency.

Finally, the principal can appoint more than one agent. However, it must be specified whether they can act individually or must act jointly. If the decision-making power is unclear it can cause confusion as well as delays when there is an emergency. My suggestion is to have one primary agent and a secondary agent, who can act as a backup should the first be unavailable, pass away first, or for any other reason be unwilling or unable to act when called upon.

The authority instilled in the agent by the Power of Attorney ceases to exist upon the principal's death. This means that the Power of Attorney can no longer act on the principal's behalf after their death. For example, the Financial Power of Attorney can no longer write checks using their authority as Power of Attorney. Upon the death of the principal, the authority shifts to the Executor or Trustee, which are roles I will explain in the next section.

ESTATE PLANNING

In addition to the legal documents that empower your advocacy, your care recipient should put in place documents that will guide the handling of their estate after they pass away. Generally, all of these documents are done at one time and are all considered a part of your care recipient's "estate plan", even though some of them are used during life.

Most people are at least familiar with the term Will. A Will (Last Will and Testament) outlines what the principal wishes to do with their assets and property after they pass away, such as leaving it to their family. A properly executed Will helps to avoid unnecessary confusion and family strife during an emotional time. Another option for transferring assets upon death is a tool called a Living Trust. With a Living Trust, the person's assets are transferred into the Trust either immediately or upon death, and it protects them from certain creditors or claims. It also allows for the avoidance of a complicated legal process called probate. The probate process is overseen by the court system, and can be both lengthy and cumbersome. As mentioned above, because a Power of Attorney is only valid while the principal is alive, it cannot be used to settle an estate or distribute assets following the principal's death. In the Trust, the principal appoints a successor Trustee, who will have the authority to step in and manage the Trust assets in event of incapacity or death without the necessity of going through the court system.

Truth be told, ensuring that your care recipient has a Will or a Living Trust set up will not make much of a difference to either of you now. But, it can make a world of difference for you after they pass away. In addition to Living Trusts, there are a lot of other different types of Trusts. Consulting with an attorney is the best way to determine if a Trust is right for you and what type would meet your needs best. I cannot promise you that doing a Trust is going to make things easy. But, it will certainly make things easier than not doing one. The most important thing to remember is that the Trust only works if the principal's assets are tied to it using beneficiary designations. If this crucial step is not done, the Trust is worth very little. Be sure to get exact instructions from the attorney assisting your care recipient on how to properly tie the assets to the Trust and ensure that your care recipient follows through with properly setting up the Trust.

Regardless of the tools that are used, a properly documented and executed estate plan that ensures your care recipient's wishes are carried out in a smooth manner will alleviate a lot of stress during an already emotional time. Many people avoid doing an estate plan because the process of putting these documents together can be overwhelming and confusing. I assure you, it is worth the effort.

Furthermore, I advise against using an online product or pulling forms from the internet and completing them yourself with a notary at the bank. It is not worth saving a few dollars to try and do it on your own. The best way to approach this is to consult with an experienced estate planning attorney who will take the time to understand your goals and wishes and then craft the documents in a clear and concise manner. Unfortunately, far too often, attorneys speak over their client's heads and the client doesn't understand what is being done for them. Recently I sat down with my maternal grandmother to review her estate documents. As she handed over a monstrous packet of papers to me, she voiced this exact concern: "I am not even sure what all of this means. The lawyer said so many things I don't understand, I just trust he got it all right because he came highly recommended." she said. Wow, I thought, I would never have wanted a client to leave the law office where I worked with a stack of documents feeling completely in the dark. If you leave the lawyer's office more confused than when you came, I recommend you move on and find another lawyer that will listen and explain in a way that makes you comfortable and confident.

STORING THE DOCUMENTS

Once the documents are finalized, they should be kept in a well-organized file in an easily accessible but secure location. I advise against using a safety deposit box to store these items, even though that is thought of as a very safe and secure location. The problem is that it is too secure. If the agent is not a signer on the safe deposit box access card, they will not be able to access it. If they are on the signature card, but do not have a key, they will still be unable to access it. And even if you have covered those bases, they will have to go through the hassle of locating and opening said box, losing precious time in the event of an emergency. It is better to keep them close at hand such as a safe inside the care recipient's home and ensuring that the agent has the code to the safe.

Be sure to give copies of the Medical Power of Attorney and Living Will or Advance Directive to your care recipient's primary care physician and other medical providers. In some states, there are online registries for storing electronic copies of these documents. The benefit to doing this is that it can provide quick access to these documents for a healthcare provider who is unfamiliar with your care recipient in an emergency situation (for example, while traveling). Many of these registries will provide a pocket card that can be carried which will easily identify the location of the online document. However, the idea of storing documents online can be unnerving for some people. Furthermore, if your care recipient makes changes to or rescinds their documents at a later date, it will be necessary to retrieve or replace these documents on the registry.

It can help to file the Financial Power of Attorney with financial institutions ahead of time. I recommend this because, even with a legal Power of Attorney, some financial institutions still will not recognize your authority and you may struggle to access their money when needed to pay for their care, services or other bills. Making sure that they are aware of and acknowledge your authority ahead of time will avoid this delay.

As important as they are, you will want to ensure that they comply with the law and will work when they need to be executed. Therefore, they should be revisited every few years to determine if any updates are needed. If anything has changed in terms of your care recipient's beneficiaries, assets or if they move to another state, they should have it updated to reflect those changes. Furthermore, the estate planning attorney will be able to advise on any law changes that may affect their estate plan.

Please heed my final piece of advice on this subject. The conversations are just as important as the documents themselves. Make sure that your care recipient talks with everyone who they name as agents and personal representatives. Being named someone's agent and not knowing it until they are called upon is an unfair and unexpected burden. Can you imagine – the hospital calls and asks you to make a care decision for someone you didn't know you were an agent for? Or the probate attorney notifies you that you are the Executor of someone's Will and you didn't know it. The agents and personal representatives should understand their role and what their responsibilities are and be given the opportunity to accept or reject it before the documents are finalized. Furthermore, they should be allowed to review the documents and ask questions. They should also know how to access the documents and other relevant information so that they will have what they need when they are expected to step into the responsibility bestowed upon them. See the checklist I have put together for this chapter to help guide you in this regard.

GUARDIANSHIP

You may be wondering whether you should pursue legal Guardianship for your care recipient. Frequently the question comes up when an older adult is not acting in their own best interests and efforts of the caregiver to use the Power of Attorney is proving unfruitful. This is a common misconception about Powers of Attorney. It cannot be used forcefully. If at any time your care recipient who is of sound mind decides they want to, they can revoke the Power of Attorney. However, if this happens and you are concerned that your care recipient is not actually competent enough to make good decisions for themselves, you will need to initiate steps to have them deemed incompetent in order to enact the Power of Attorney. Unfortunately, if they are making bad decisions and do have capacity, there isn't much you can do. In more dire situations, especially if you feel they are a potential harm to self or others, taking the step towards establishing Guardianship may be warranted.

If they did not execute Power of Attorney documents prior to becoming incapacitated, it may be necessary for you to be named their Guardian to act and advocate for them. Technically, there are two roles– Guardianship (the responsibility for the care of the physical person) and Conservatorship (the responsibility for the finances of the person). Usually, but not always, they are given to the same person to act on the care recipient's behalf but they can be given to two different people. Being a Guardian is a large responsibility, as is being an agent under Power of Attorney. The biggest difference between the two is that being a Guardian involves being supervised by the courts while Power of Attorney does not.

Guardianship, I know, sounds terrible. That is because it is! It is a complicated and expensive process that involves a lot of legal documentation and interaction with the courts. It can be intimidating and is easy to misstep without legal counsel (which of course, makes it more expensive). Moreover, it is an extreme measure because it is truly the legal termination of the care recipient's rights. It should not be taken lightly. It should be used only as a last resort when there isn't a good alternative. The ideal scenario in my opinion is the care recipient choosing their trusted agents ahead of time and empowering them to support them when they lose capacity. One of the best ways to empower the agents is to set up a supportive team of professionals to help.

CALLING IN REINFORCEMENTS

Even with the legal authority to act on behalf of your care recipient, the problem many people face is locating and securing the type of care services and support they need when they need it. You cannot be expected to become an expert in all things caregiving overnight! So start with the E in the GUESS acronym and begin to educate yourself.

To start, there are several community resources that you can tap into to glean information on the resources available in your area. The local Area Agency on Aging is a good place to start. Eldercare Locator is another resource for aging adults provided through a partnership of the Area Agencies on Aging and the U.S. Administration on Aging (AoA). This is a resource for services such as legal and financial services, home health care, home renovations, and transportation. You can contact the Eldercare Locator by calling 800-677-1116 or by visiting their website.

Locating resources that are specific to the disease or illness that your care recipient lives with will be vital to managing your care recipient's care needs in the home setting long term. To find these resources, you can ask their doctor, the social work department at your local hospital, local nonprofit organizations, or check the National Institutes of Health website. Many communities across the country also have Programs of All-Inclusive Care for the Elderly (PACE®) programs to assist aging adults with care coordination. PACE can be contacted by calling 1-800-MEDICARE or by visiting their website.

I have found that most caregivers fall loosely into two categories — the ones that need guidance and consultation but still want to "do" and manage everything on their own; and others that need someone to hand hold them every step of the way. Regardless of which category you fall into, even if all the necessary information were to just magically appear at your fingertips, it can be difficult to decipher it all and determine what is needed. Would you diagnose yourself if you are not a doctor? Build a house if you are not a builder? The answer (hopefully) is probably no. Caregiving is no different. Don't expend all of your resources attempting to navigate the complicated world of senior care on your own. Instead, adhere to the "S" in the GUESS acronym- seek out and engage with professionals and experts who can support you. One of the most effective ways to advocate for your care recipient is to build a team of professionals around you that can give skilled, caring guidance when you encounter situations you are unfamiliar with and provide lifelines to you at the times you need them. I like to call this close support network your "advocacy team".

My advice is to start by finding a "coach" for the advocacy team - someone who can not only provide you with their own expertise, but also help you locate and vet other professionals who specialize in the varying types of support you may need. This "coach" should be a professional in the area of elder care or gerontology. I do want to make a clear distinction here because making this determination can be confusing. I do not mean for example, hiring a home care agency and relying on the manager or care coordinator to give you advice. Titles used for varying positions within the senior healthcare industry can imply a level of expertise at times can be misleading. This is not done to intentionally mislead people but rather to impart a sense of trust and assurance. While there are plenty of caring people who work in this field and are willing to help, what I am referring to is hiring a professional who works for you and your care recipient as an advocate. This ensures that they are primarily motivated to advocate for your care recipient's well being, and have no intentional or unintentional conflicting motives. This person should possess a combination of education, experience, and credentials in the field of gerontology. Gerontology simply put is the study of aging. There are a number of different professional designations and certifications one can get. It seems more are available every year, as senior care is a rapidly growing field. As I mentioned, I am a Certified Aging Life Care Manager. This relatively new and quickly evolving field is known as Aging Life Care Management. Aging Life Care Managers vary in education, background and skills, but a common thread amongst the profession is advocacy. They act as a hub for communication, a counselor regarding unfamiliar topics, and most importantly, a voice for their clients. Enlisting the help of an Aging Life Care Manager to help you navigate the process is most beneficial from the beginning so that you do not spend precious time and energy looking in the wrong places for the resources and guidance you need. You can search for an Aging Life Care Manager in your area on the Association's website.[8] If you have a difficult time finding one, there are other types of professionals that you can seek out, such as a Geriatric Social Worker or a Certified Senior Advisor.

As I mentioned, there are other types of senior care professionals that could help you, and some of them should be a part of your advocacy team. But I recommend you start by seeking an Aging Life Care Professional. You can rest assured that an Aging Life Care Professional meets the criteria and standards of the industry. According to the standards of the profession, the client is the care recipient and is the center of the complex "system" they are a part of.[9] All services must be considered in the context of this system and their relationships. You, the caregiver, may have initiated the engagement with the care manager and may even be paying for the services, but bear in mind the care recipient is

---

[8] aginglifecare.org
[9] https://www.aginglifecare.org/ALCAWEB/About%20Us/Code_of_Ethics_and_Standards_of_Practice/ALCAWEB/ About_Us/Code_of_Ethics_and_Standards_of_Practice.aspx?hkey=4808b101-6f91-4a47-bd3e-b7e91e7285d6

always the client and the focus. Furthermore, there are any number of individuals who are involved in the client's "system". They can include informal (unpaid) and formal (paid) caregivers, family, friends, neighbors, community representatives, government and agency representatives, and an array of other professionals that you may find helpful as counselors in the aging care journey. Please always remember how important it is that your care recipient remains an integrated part of the team at all times. I want you to take this very seriously. Do not cut them out of decision-making. Multiple studies have shown that people with greater self-determination are more independent, enjoy better mental health, remain more integrated into their communities, and are less susceptible to abuse and exploitation. The more they remain involved, the more comfortable they will be with the plan. Even when your care recipient begins to exhibit a loss of decision-making abilities, you can keep them involved by giving them structured choices, focusing on their strengths, and using the safest but least restrictive approaches to help them. Each member of the team will all be able to provide crucial advice based on their area of expertise and assist your care recipient with proactive planning, identifying and pulling together resources, and providing impartial guidance when navigating challenges. Planning ahead for future care can keep the care recipient in control, even if capacity issues develop later.

Additionally, having an advocacy team provides checks and balances. This is important because your care recipient will become more vulnerable over time. For any one individual person to have full access is setting your care recipient up for the potential of abuse of that power. Conversely, having a qualified team of professionals looking out for their best interest will greatly reduce the risks.

Once you have your "coach", they can help you build out the rest of your advocacy team. Depending on your situation, you may need varying types of professionals to support you at different times in your journey. Your team could look very different than a friend who is also caring for an aging adult. Your team should be thoroughly vetted and routinely revisited to ensure that they are being proactive and always doing what is right by your care recipient. It is important to remember that no two caregiving journeys are exactly alike, but I do believe this team concept is beneficial and should be utilized by all caregivers. To get you started, I have put together a guide for this chapter to help you with building your advocacy team.

NECESSARY LEGAL DOCUMENTS

This checklist outlines the documents your care recipient needs*, and that they are less than 5 years old:

- ☐ Will or Trust
- ☐ Living Will/Advance Directive
- ☐ HIPAA Release (the Living Will/Advance Directive may include this)
- ☐ Medical Power of Attorney
- ☐ Financial Power of Attorney

What to do with the documents:

- ☐ Discuss them– ensure a clear understanding of what is being expected of you as the agent, and how your care recipient wants you to act on their behalf when they cannot speak for themselves
- ☐ Give copies of the Living Will/Advance Directive and Medical Power of Attorney to the medical providers
- ☐ Give a copy of the Financial Power of attorney to banks and financial institutions
- ☐ Check to see if your care recipient's state offers an online registries the Living Wills/Advance Medical Directives
- ☐ If they have a DNR, put it on the refrigerator
- ☐ Store the originals in a secure but accessible place
- ☐ Review them at least every 5 years

*You should consult with an attorney for advice specific to your care recipient's situation.

GUIDANCE FOR FINANCIAL AGENTS

This guide will provide guidance for those who are serving as a financial Power of Attorney.

- Be an authorized signer, not a joint account holder.

- Do not co-mingle funds of yours or anyone else's.

- The agent should keep a written record of expenses paid.

- The agent should never borrow from the account.

- The agent should always write reasons for the expense in the memo of the checks.

- The agent should keep detailed records and be transparent with others involved in the care recipient's care.

- Work with your care recipient's financial advisors and bankers to stay on top of cash flow and financial projections.

- For agents who are being paid as a caregiver to the principal, there should be a well-organized agreement between the two outlining the terms of the arrangements. The agent should not be writing checks to themselves.

- Agents should never attempt to influence their care recipient's plans for distributing assets upon their death.

- If there are ever conflicts or discrepancies, seek impartial counsel right away.

VITAL INFORMATION FOR AGENTS
AND PERSONAL REPRESENTATIVES

This checklist outlines the pertinent information you should have (or know how to gain access to), as an agent or personal representative. This information will allow you to more easily identify your care recipient and validate your authority, and advocate effectively for them.

Personal Information:
- Full legal name including middle names, maiden or previous names, and aliases
- Date of birth
- Place of birth
- Parents names
- Social Security Number
- Medicare/insurance policy numbers

Financial Information:
- Important contacts:
  - Attorney(s)
  - Banker(s)
  - Financial Advisor(s)
  - Insurance agent(s)
    - Personal Property and Casualty
    - Life
    - Health
    - Disability
    - Long term care
- Location of Important Legal Documents
- Insurance policy information
- Bank accounts
- Net worth statement
- Household finance information

· Location of safety deposit boxes

Household Information:
- Utility contacts:
  - > Water
  - > Gas
  - > Electric
  - > Other
- Maintenance contacts:
  - > Maid services
  - > Lawn care
  - > Laundry Service
  - > General maintenance
  - > Other
- Location of appliance records/manuals
- Pet information
- Alarm/security codes or passwords

PUTTING TOGETHER YOUR ADVOCACY TEAM

This Guide includes individuals and professionals to be considered for inclusion when putting together the Advocacy Team.

The primary types of professionals I recommend hiring for your Advocacy team include:
- Medical/Healthcare: Physicians, specialists, geriatric mental health counselor or licensed clinical social worker, *Aging Life Care Manager, Pharmacists
- Legal: Elder law attorney, Estate Planning Attorney
- Financial: Bankers, financial advisor, CPA

*The Aging Life Care Manager or similarly credentialed professional should serve as your "coach". Seek out this person first.

A secondary list (these may not be necessary, they may be necessary only for a short time, or they may be interchangeable with others listed above, depending on your situation):
- Bookkeeper or Daily Money Manager
- Medicare expert and/or insurance specialist
- Home health care professionals, therapists
- A Seniors Real Estate Specialist
- A Senior Move Manager
- An Aging in Place Specialist
- Senior Living Placement Specialist
- You may need other types of legal counsel for specific situations

NOTES

NOTES

CHAPTER 2

THE MEDICAL

*It's not about how much you do but how much love
you put into the doing.*
-Mother Theresa

AILMENTS OF THE AGING POPULATION

It can be difficult to recognize that your care recipient is beginning to decline medically or mentally. However, the longer we live, the more susceptible we are to chronic illnesses. In fact, according to the CDC, six in ten older adults have at least one chronic medical condition. Most of these conditions, If well controlled and monitored by a physician, can be managed for quite some time without any drastic effects on quality of life. But, a progressive diagnosis such as Alzheimer's disease, arthritis, COPD, CHF, or diabetes, can cause dramatic debilitation over time. Many older adults struggle to manage these illnesses properly without assistance. They are often faced with more challenges in managing daily life. Furthermore, navigating the healthcare system is extremely challenging, and those living with chronic illnesses must interact with the healthcare system on a more regular basis.

Chronic illnesses can limit mobility, cause pain and significantly reduce quality of life. As these diseases progress, the symptoms and the side effects of medications used to manage them can take a dramatic toll. You may notice they begin to affect your care recipient's ability to maintain their self care and their household responsibilities. The pace of the progression towards disability varies widely depending on the individual, but even the most common ailments such as hearing and vision loss can drastically change the landscape of their independent life.

Oftentimes older adults will experience difficulties with performing what is referred to as Activities of Daily Living (ADLs) and Instrumental Activities of Daily Living (IADLs). IADLs include activities related to living independently, such as managing finances and cooking. These usually begin to falter first, and it often goes unrecognized by family and friends because they are not as obvious. ADLs are activities related to personal hygiene and daily functioning, such as bathing and dressing. The ability to perform both ADLs and IADLs is vital to self-care and independence. If your care recipient becomes unable to perform these activities satisfactorily and safely, they may no longer be able to live independently without support from you or others.

Rest assured that the role of caregiving does not mean you have to become a nurse overnight. There are a variety of resources that you can rely on to do the heavy lifting when it comes to your care recipient's medical care. There are very important reasons that setting boundaries is one of my top five tips for caregivers. One of those reasons is that knowing when you are crossing into the zone of discomfort will help you recognize when it is time to start making other arrangements for your care recipient's care. When that happens, call upon the professionals in your advocacy team for guidance and referrals.

What boundaries am I referring to? Mainly, I mean the activities of daily living. Many people are comfortable assisting with IADLs, but once the line is crossed to the more personal zone of ADLs such as toileting and bathing, they find themselves uncomfortable. This discomfort is likely to be stronger for some types of relationships than others. Regardless, it is an acceptable way to feel; you do not have to feel guilty because you want to keep some respectful boundaries of privacy between you and your care recipient. To help you with this I have put together a boundaries checklist that will help you assess what your limits are and when to call in reinforcements for help.

You must also determine what you are able and willing to do from a medical standpoint. For example, to manage chronic illnesses effectively, many older adults with chronic illnesses often take a laundry list of medications. I remember the first few times I was responsible for entering the medication lists into the charts for new residents to the nursing facility where I worked. The lists were a half dozen or more pages long! I was shocked. Numerous complications can occur when medications are not managed properly and it can become a cumbersome task for caregivers. In addition to medications, many older adults have other medical instructions they must follow to stay healthy. For example, managing diabetes can include checking blood sugar regularly and in many instances administering insulin. Some people with osteoporosis also receive regular injections of medications designed to maintain bone density. If your care recipient becomes unable to do this on their own, you will need to consider if you are comfortable with giving these injections. And even if you are, is the frequency they are required on a schedule you can maintain? This can be very challenging.

Furthermore, your care recipient's care plan may include certain dietary restrictions and exercise routines. Even in the absence of medical restrictions, a healthy lifestyle includes proper nutrition and hydration which are important at all ages but become even more necessary as we age. Unfortunately, many older adults do not eat well and fall into unhealthy habits. Those who live alone may feel it is not worth the effort to cook healthy meals only for themselves, and they can easily fall into the trap of eating unhealthy convenience meals loaded with preservatives and sodium. Be sure to keep an eye on the type of diet your care recipient is following. Healthy eating is critical for their health and you may find that you need to remind and encourage them to comply. One of the most common requests for home care assistance is for meal preparation. You may want to consider engaging with a home care company to provide this service if your care recipient is struggling in this area. Another way to ensure your care recipient is getting healthy, safely prepared meals is to enroll them in a Meals on Wheels program through the local Area Agency on Aging. This is a federally funded program that ensures home-bound seniors receive nutritious meals, delivered by volunteers. It is also beneficial to have an extra set of eyes checking in on your care recipient through this program. The USDA offers a wealth of information regarding nutrition for older adults on their website.[10]

Once you have established your boundaries, it is a good idea to seek some training on the tasks that may be required of you. Most informal caregivers do not start off with the skills necessary to care for an aging adult. However, you can learn the basics about providing hands-on care pretty easily through the Area Agency on Aging, local nonprofits, or caregiving schools. You may even be able to utilize Medicare to pay for training by a home health professional. Start by asking your care recipient's physician for recommendations.

Furthermore, being well informed and knowledgeable about your care recipient's medical conditions allows you to be vigilant when symptoms arise and able to inform the medical professionals of what is going on. This keeps you in a proactive stance, significantly reducing the likelihood of a life-altering medical event catching you off-guard. In addition to education from your care recipient's physicians, you may also want to look into chronic illness classes and support groups. For example, local hospitals often offer classes for people living with chronic illnesses. When I was diagnosed with gestational diabetes when pregnant with my first child, I was able to take advantage of the pregnancy nutrition classes and support group offered through my local hospital that were covered by my insurance. This is often the case for many types of illnesses and diseases. You can also contact your local Area Agency on Aging for information on other resources available through other community groups and organizations. Don't hesitate to engage your advocacy team for help with this. We will also cover in a later chapter about resources to engage if you find additional support is needed.

NAVIGATING HEALTHCARE

As a caregiver and advocate, navigating the healthcare system is a vital

---

[10] www.nutrition.gov/topics/nutrition-life-stage/older-adults

function of your role. The healthcare system is so disjointed that the lack of communication and information sharing can make for an extremely troublesome health care experience even with well-meaning healthcare providers. Furthermore, oftentimes caregivers find themselves thrust into the advocacy role when their care recipient is not treated fairly by the medical community due to unfortunate ageism that exists within the healthcare system.

The first step is to remember the "U" in the GUESS acronym – understanding your care recipient. Along with the Medical Power of Attorney and Living Will or Advance Directive we discussed earlier, you will need to be prepared with the basic demographic information you may need to identify your care recipient and answer questions from medical providers. For example, know your care recipient's full legal name, date of birth, location of birth, Social Security number, and primary care provider's name and phone number. You should also be aware of their known allergies, primary diagnosis, medical history and blood type. Always have a medication list that is kept current. The more you know about your care recipient's medical condition and baseline, the better equipped you will be to answer medical providers' questions and the more comfortable you will be making care decisions. See the checklist on this subject for more guidance.

One way to ensure quality, seamless care for your care recipient is to ensure that they have an established primary care physician (PCP) who they see on a regular basis and who is competent in the ailments and needs of the aging population. Many older adults only visit their specialists (such as a cardiologist or pulmonologist), and while their specialists are likely skilled and competent physicians, they are treating an individual diagnosis, and therefore not looking at the patient as a whole. By maintaining an ongoing relationship with a PCP who serves as the "hub", the patient ensures that someone is putting all of the pieces together and looking at things in the "big picture". Think of the PCP as a part of your Advocacy team. Attend your care recipient's medical appointments when you are able, so that you can stay up to date. Ask the doctor to help you by keeping medication and treatment plans as simple and easy to follow as possible. When possible, align medication schedules to minimize the number of times per day you are required to administer medications. While some medications have more specific rules for time frames for when they should be given, with the doctor's help you can somewhat customize the plan to you and your care recipient's schedules and ensure that it is as manageable as possible.

Keeping a log or journal is a great way to stay organized regarding your care recipient's medical condition. There are many things to track and it can be hard to do without a written diary. The resources for this chapter include a sample log, but you can also keep track by using an app, whatever is easiest for you. However you do it, don't keep it to yourself! Share your record keeping with your care recipient's primary care physician. Reviewing it with them will help you and your care recipient's doctors identify patterns and what may trigger flare ups or certain symptoms. This type of tracking can be time consuming, but it can be extremely helpful when you are trying to get your arms around what is going wrong when your care recipient is showing a decline. This can make a significant difference in maximizing your care recipient's quality of life.

All of this is a lot to keep up with! Navigating medical appointments and working to keep all of the information in order is an uphill battle, especially if your care recipient has chronic conditions and sees multiple specialists. I have also put together a list of questions for doctor's visits that may help you make the most of the limited but crucial time you will have with your care recipient's medical providers. Be sure to write down the answers and keep track of the recommendations made by their providers. This is a key strategy to understanding their medical condition and care needs.

Problems can arise when the PCP is left out of the loop when the patient utilizes other parts of the medical system, such as a hospital or skilled nursing facility. Sometimes the PCP doesn't even know about the hospital admission, and often no one communicates with them about what is going on with their patient. Keeping your care recipient's PCP well informed may fall on your shoulders, and is critical to ensure the best quality of care possible. Always request that copies of medical records be sent to the primary care physician at the end of a hospital visit, and always insist upon good communication between providers caring for your care recipient.

This leads to the concern about the lack of shared electronic medical records. As your care recipient ages they may begin to experience more frequent hospitalizations. This can result in a hefty volume of disjointed medical records. Considering that many older adults are often unreliable when it comes to accurate reporting due to cognitive impairments, difficulty hearing or simply not understanding medical jargon, the problem is exacerbated. This can cause them to retain only minimal information about their medical conditions and plan of care. This is why your role as an advocate is so important when it comes to their medical care.

When they are in the hospital, ensuring that a seamless flow of communication happens between the different departments and providers you come into contact with is vitally important. I emphasize that it may be up to you to ensure this happens. Communication breakdowns are a primary cause of mistakes leading to poor care, injuries, and even death in hospitals. This is most important when your care recipient is transitioned from one level of care to the next. Without this communication, hospital physicians and staff are less likely to be able to make informed decisions, and more likely to make mistakes. Remember, there is no such thing as a dumb question! If you are unsure about something, ask. This is the best way to ensure that the communication is effective. It is imperative to ensure that your questions are answered fully each step of the way. In doing so, you will be prepared to make informed decisions and communicate effectively with the next provider you come into contact with.

Furthermore, older adults frequently experience confusion and decreased cognitive functioning while hospitalized. The mental deterioration your care recipient may experience while in the hospital can be the result of many varying factors, from exhaustion and stress to medication side effects, effects from anesthesia, dehydration, or delirium otherwise related to their acute medical condition. (To combat this, visit them as much as you can, and bring them items to help keep them occupied such as books, crafts, crossword puzzles, and the like. If you cannot be there, consider using a virtual call to check in so that they get to see your face). Because of this, sometimes doctors that do not know the patient well will reference the confusion as dementia in the chart. Unfortunately, once this has been done, it is very hard to erase! While the type of delirium that is experienced in the hospital will usually resolve itself once the acute medical problem has been treated, dementia is a long term condition. Receiving an inaccurate label of dementia can be problematic for your care recipient for a number of reasons, and it is important to address and have it stricken from the medical record as soon as possible if it happens.

To overcome this challenge, first, it is very important to review the medical records from a hospitalization. You want to do this to ensure accuracy and completeness. These records will have an influence on treatment plans, rehabilitative care planning, nursing facility admission decisions, billing and more. The consistency and quality of your care recipient's care is at stake. Request the medical records upon or as soon after discharge as possible, and bear in mind that providers are required by law to make this information available to you within 30 days of the request. You may be required to make this request in writing and there may be a charge. As I mentioned earlier, you want to ensure that your care recipient's PCP receives a copy also. If you find a discrepancy or omission that you feel was an error, bring it to the attention of the medical facility administration and your insurance company as soon as possible.

Second, recall my earlier statement about the Health Insurance Portability and Accountability Act (HIPAA). Be aware of what this Act really does. Its rules and protections are widely misinterpreted and misused by medical professionals. HIPAA was enacted to ensure that providers safeguard your Protected Health Information (PHI), which is your individually identifiable health information such as demographic information, contact information, diagnosis, test results, and treatment plans as they store and transmit that information. What HIPAA is not in existence to do is prevent doctors from talking to patient's families and caregivers. However, they occasionally use it as a shield. This hurdle is why I recommended including a HIPAA release in your care recipient's Advanced Directive. If you are ever in a situation in which a provider refuses to talk to you or provide you with information you are requesting as it relates to your care recipient's treatment or care plan, citing HIPAA as the reason, knowing the specifics of this law can be very helpful. They do say you catch more flies with honey and while maintaining a pleasant demeanor can go a long way, do not back down if you are not getting what you need. If your care recipient's providers simply don't step up to the plate, don't hesitate to find new ones.

Another area that is particularly challenging is medication reconciliation. When your care recipient is discharged from the hospital, it is imperative that you reconcile their medications when you get home. Home health companies usually offer this service, but sometimes you'll need to explicitly ask for it. Make sure that your care recipient does not just go home and resume their prior medication routine while disregarding the changes made in the hospital. In the eight years I operated a home care company, this was by far the most frequent mistake we found during our first home visit after a hospitalization. Without a comprehensive review and reconciliation, your care recipient could end up taking old medications that have been discharged, taking the wrong dose of a medication they should be taking, or not getting new medications filled that have been started in the hospital. This can be extremely dangerous, life threatening even.

A good example of this is one of my home care clients, Valerie. Valerie was in her early 90s and lived alone with the help of a caregiver every day for four hours each day. The caregiver made sure Valerie was clean and dressed, took her medications, and had a hot meal for lunch. They often went shopping and enjoyed other outings together. Valerie was in good shape for a woman in her 90s, but she took a lot of medications. After a hospitalization for a fall, which thankfully did not result in serious injury, Valerie was discharged with an order for physical therapy and new prescriptions. She and her caregiver filled the prescriptions promptly and returned home. The discharging physician at the hospital had given her a prescription for a heart medication that she routinely takes and therefore she filled the prescription even though she still had a bottle of the same medication at home. Thankfully, the next morning her caregiver noticed this and brought it to management's attention. The nurse contacted Valerie's physician and resolved the issue quickly. If it had not been for the vigilant observation of the caregiver, this situation could have had dire consequences as taking too much of this medication could have been very dangerous.

Elderly patients (particularly those who live alone) are extremely susceptible to mistakes such as this slipping through the cracks. Be vigilant when it comes to comparing the medications your care recipient is discharged with and what they are taking at home and ensure that their primary care physician is notified of any changes that occurred while in the hospital.

"AMA"

I think anyone who has been there will agree – a stay in the hospital is certainly no vacation. It is uncomfortable, noisy, and difficult to get any rest. Your care recipient is likely to be sleep deprived and agitated. Not to mention probably hungry because the food is subpar to say the least. They are also likely to decline both physically and mentally as they are lying in the hospital bed for most of the time and lack any mental stimulation.

For these aforementioned reasons, an older adult may be inclined to leave the hospital even before they are medically ready. I have also experienced that more often than not, the hospital is more than happy to discharge sooner than later as it reduces the overall costs on the system. One tactic that they will often take is to suggest the patient sign themselves out "Against Medical Advice" (AMA). This term means that the patient is acknowledging that he or she may not be medically stable for discharge but is leaving anyway. They will ask the patient to sign a form acknowledging this, in an attempt to alleviate themselves from any legal responsibility. By doing this, the hospital and providers also have certain protections against malpractice claims should the patient get worse or pass away after leaving the hospital. If you or your care recipient are asked to sign such a form, be sure that you document your reasons for deciding to do so and keep copies of all of the documentation from the hospital stay.

In my experience, there is a lot of misinformation being given out in regard to AMA discharges. One inaccuracy often communicated by medical providers to patients is that should they decide to leave the hospital AMA, insurance will not cover the services provided. This is not the case, and if they do ask you or your care recipient to sign something stating that you will be financially responsible for your medical bills, *do not do it*. Keep in mind that your care recipient (and all patients) is protected by other federal laws. For example, a patient always has the right to informed consent and right to refuse treatment. This means that the providers your care recipient interacts with should always explain the risks and benefits of any proposed treatment and ensure that they understand the implications of the decision they are making. Once they understand those risks and benefits, if your care recipient is competent, they have the right to refuse any treatment they do not want. If they are incompetent, as their agent you will have the right to make these decisions.

Another misconception is that when a patient discharges AMA, they are not allowed to provide any post-discharge instructions or assist with arranging post-discharge services. If your care recipient is insistent upon leaving the hospital AMA, you still have the right to receive important discharge instructions, including physician orders for medications or treatments. It never made sense to me why a medical facility would refuse to do so, as providing this information is clearly a better way to avoid negative post-discharge outcomes and therefore protect the providers against claims of negligence. However, much like the way HIPAA is used as a shield when a provider does not want to deal with a demanding caregiver, I have seen this "policy" used in this fashion countless times. It is a copout and unacceptable.

Please take note that I am not advocating for your care recipient to push to be discharged before they are medically stable. If you find yourself in a situation where your care recipient is insisting upon leaving when the doctors are not recommending it, do your best to encourage them to stay until medically cleared for discharge. This is the safest route for all involved. However, regardless of whether your care recipient is leaving the hospital with physician clearance, or without, as their caregiver and advocate you should insist upon having your specific questions answered so that you can be fully prepared for the transition home. In fact, about 38 states* and the District of Columbia have the CARE (Caregiver Advise, Record, Enable) Act (not to be confused with the CARES Act, which was a stimulus bill related to the Coronavirus).[11] The CARE Act was enacted as a measure to improve upon the often hurried and deficient hospital discharge process. The Act requires that hospitals perform the following three steps during every hospital discharge:

---

[11] The CARE Act Implementation: Progress and Promise Susan C. Reinhard AARP Public Policy Institute Heather M. Young Betty Irene Moore School of Nursing, UC Davis Elaine Ryan AARP State Advocacy & Strategy Integration Rita B. Choula AARP Public Policy Institute

- Identify the primary caregiver of the patient.

- Inform the primary caregiver when the patient is cleared for discharge.

- Provide the caregiver with education and training on how to perform the medical care that the patient will need for their post-acute care.

Clearly, the key element here is the requirement that caregivers are educated and trained when their care recipient is being discharged with new medical needs. This could include things like operating medical equipment (IVs, oxygen, etc.), giving injections, dressing wounds, and even more complex activities. Most informal caregivers lack medical training and skills and therefore are relying heavily on the medical community to assist them with learning and performing these tasks. But, unless they speak up (which many are hesitant or don't know how to do), the education on how to perform these tasks is usually minimal or glossed over if addressed at all. In my experience, even working and living in a state with the CARE Act, it hasn't made a big impact. So, caregivers need to be vocal about what they need to feel confident and comfortable in caring for their care recipients once they return home.

Unfortunately, Medicare does not pay for the caregiver education and instruction; however, it is the responsibility of the hospital in the states that have the Act to ensure that this education is provided, at their own cost. However, simply knowing that this Act applies to you and speaking up about it could turn the tides in your direction in terms of getting the support you need from the hospital staff. You can even go so far as to carry a visual representation, keeping it with your care recipient's important medical and legal documents. This visual item is a wallet card designed by AARP – available to download for free on their website.[12]

I may sound like a broken record, but if any of your questions have not been fully answered or if you have concerns about your care recipient going home, *don't be afraid to speak up!* Ask your questions again and again until you get them answered to your satisfaction before the day of discharge. Make sure that both you and your care recipient are comfortable with the plans and discharge

---

[12] aarp.org

recommendations. Safety is of utmost importance, and you should have your concerns about the discharge plan addressed before leaving. You can receive a wealth of other resources and information from the hospital's discharge planner or case manager. You can also use the hospital discharge checklist I put together for this chapter to guide you.

Fortunately, hospital systems do recognize that ensuring that services such as elder in-home care are set up can make a huge difference in the patient's overall success. They are not blind to the data that is out there. Some hospitals, as a response to Medicare penalties for readmission, are even implementing programs that include monitoring of the patient post-discharge. In such programs nurse discharge navigators are assigned to check in with the patient in the community and services offered include things like follow-up appointment coordination, appointment reminder calls, and resource connection. Make the most of these check-ins, asking questions if you need help. If implemented appropriately these discharge navigation efforts could be extremely beneficial in ensuring elders are successful in achieving their post-discharge goals. But this is a small step towards a solution for a gigantic and rapidly growing problem.

States that have enacted the CARE Act: Alaska, Arkansas, California, Colorado, Connecticut, Delaware, Hawaii, Illinois, Indiana, Iowa, Kansas, Kentucky, Louisiana, Maine, Maryland, Massachusetts, Michigan, Mississippi, Missouri, Montana, Nebraska, Nevada, New Hampshire, New Jersey, New Mexico, New York, North Dakota, Ohio, Oklahoma, Oregon, Pennsylvania, Rhode Island, Texas, Utah, Virginia, Washington, West Virginia, and Wyoming as well as the District of Columbia, the U.S. Virgin Islands and Puerto Rico.

PATIENT ADVOCATES

If you are having any difficulty at all receiving or understanding what you need from the providers or discharge planning team, a good resource can be the patient advocate. On staff at many hospitals are patient advocates whose job is to ensure patients receive a quality experience in their facility and step in when perhaps they are not. While the clinicians and providers don't always have the time to explain everything to your satisfaction, patient advocates do just that. Do keep in mind that patient advocates are usually nurse case managers who are a part of the "risk management" department. That means that while they should have your best interest at heart (and probably do or they wouldn't be doing this type of work), they are still ultimately working to avoid the hospital facing any legal trouble. If the hospital doesn't have a patient advocate, or you feel you aren't getting what you need from them, contact your care recipient's insurance company to see if they can provide one. In some cases, medical insurance will cover and/or provide a private patient advocate for their members. If not, as mentioned earlier you can also hire an Aging Life Care Manager to serve as an advocate; however, insurance coverage for this type of service is slim to none so the expense for that will likely be out of pocket.

Finally, keep your expectations realistic. Your care recipient is not likely to return to their baseline ability as soon as they return home. They may have a long journey of rehabilitation and nursing care ahead of them. Ask the discharging physician for an expected length of recovery time, but also verify those expectations with the home health providers after they have assessed your care recipient and have a care plan in place.

SHORT-TERM REHABILITATION

In situations where your care recipient's physical condition has deteriorated drastically during the hospital stay, it may be recommended that they not go straight home. Instead, it might be recommended that they go either an acute or subacute rehab center for short term rehabilitation. What is short term rehabilitation? It means receiving therapy services for a short period of time (usually 1-3 months) in a facility that provides medical oversight. The therapy they will receive may include a combination of physical, occupational and/or speech therapy depending on the type of illness or injury they had and the condition they are in. The idea is that they will regain strength and mobility while receiving 24-hour care and supervision to keep them safe and stable medically. Doing so will presumably increase the chances that they are able to return to their home setting safely and with a lower likelihood of returning to the hospital. There is a significant amount of data which backs up this claim, which is why Medicare is so willing to pay for it, since reducing hospital readmissions (and therefore costs) is the primary motivator.

If the medical professionals suggest it, I highly recommend your care recipient go. But, there is a good chance that they are not going to want to go. I spent six years working mostly in the admissions department in a skilled nursing facility and I am here to tell you that nine out of ten new residents did not want to be there! It is important to approach this with a realistic point of view. Whether it is an acute or sub-acute facility doesn't make too much of a difference in the setting. It is going to be hospital-like either way. There will be call bells ringing, overhead pages happening, and lots of hustle and bustle going on. It is not a restful, relaxing place to be. This can be very disconcerting, especially during the first experience. However, a stay in an acute rehab is usually easier because it is shorter and the other patients there are there for the same reason. With sub-acute rehabilitation in a skilled nursing facility, the experience is different. Generally, the population consists of both short term and long term residents. This can be off-putting for a short term resident to see long term residents in severely debilitated mental and physical conditions. It can be hard on their spirits, to feel as if they are being taken to a "nursing home". It is also good to be prepared for what the rooms will be like. Generally, they are small and contain hospital-like furnishings. And while the trend in the newer facilities is going against this, it is likely that your care recipient will have to share a room and bathroom with another resident. You cannot expect much in the way of privacy in these facilities.

Acute and subacute rehab centers differ in some key ways. At an acute rehab center they will have a more rigorous therapy program and will need to be able to tolerate at least three hours of intense rehab each day. The stay is relatively short (usually less than a month). The most common type of facility that offers subacute rehabilitation is known as a skilled nursing facility (SNF- yes, it's said like *sniff*!). At a SNF, they will only be expected to participate in 1-2 hours of rehab each day. And while some SNF facilities offer therapy on the weekend, not all do, while in an acute rehab there will be therapy provided 7 days per week. But, there is around the clock nursing care provided at both. In general, but not always, it is usually recommended that the frail elderly go to a sub-acute facility because their tolerance for therapy participation is not likely to be sufficient for the level of intensity at an acute rehab. This really depends on how debilitated they are after their illness or injury. The stay in a SNF is usually longer because it takes longer to rehab a frailer patient.

In an acute rehab center, there will be doctors rounding every day. This is because they are licensed as a hospital and this is a requirement. At subacute rehab, the doctors do not necessarily visit daily. Also, the nursing staff to patient ratio is much higher than that of an acute facility. But, because SNFs house both short-term and long-term residents, there are additional support services in a SNF that you generally will not find in an acute rehab, such as robust activity programs.

Ultimately, the doctor's recommendation (along with the recommendations from the therapists that may have worked with them while they are in the hospital) and insurance's approval will determine which level of care is appropriate for your care recipient and therefore which type of facility they will be transferred to. However, remember your care recipient should have a choice for the location in which to receive this rehabilitation, within the limits of which ones their insurance will pay for. The hospital should look into this for you and provide you with a list. These facilities vary greatly in terms of the level and quality of care provided, and the hospitals do not do the due diligence for you. While the savvy hospital discharge planner may point you in the right direction by circling or highlighting the facilities they would most highly recommend, they are bound by hospital policies and regulations not to influence patient decisions. Therefore, they should give you ample time to do your research. But often, and unfortunately, you are forced to make this decision with not much more than a moment's notice. Sometimes, even the same day of discharge. *Get ready to advocate!* Do not hesitate to insist upon additional time to do this vetting. A safe discharge plan is a requirement for hospital regulations, and if you push back to request time to make safe discharge arrangements, they are likely to comply. This will give you time to visit the facilities and determine which one would be the best choice for your care recipient.

How do you choose the right one? When you are faced with a quick decision, the most important things are the following:

- Location

- CMS 5 Star Rating[13]

- Reviews from past residents

These three factors are the most important. The first one is critical because the closer your care recipient is to you, the more you can visit which will make a large impact on their recovery. The second and third are going to give you the most insight into what your care recipient is likely to experience as a resident there. If you are able to schedule a physical tour prior to your care recipient's hospital transfer, pay attention to cleanliness and the appearance of other residents. Don't pay as much attention to the physical appearance of the building (as long as everything seems in good working condition and no safety hazards, the "aesthetics" are not as important). You may also want to locate and briefly interview some of the providers (therapists/nurses/physicians) to get a better feel for who your care recipient will be working with.

Once your care recipient is settled into a rehab facility, you should be prepared with realistic expectations regarding the length of stay that Medicare will cover. Most people believe that Medicare will pay for 100 days in a skilled nursing facility. This is a common misunderstanding. Following a qualifying three-night hospital stay, Medicare will pay for *up to* 20 days in a SNF at 100 percent and *up to* 80 more days with a co-pay. Furthermore, if your care recipient has another type of insurance such as Medicare Advantage, the coverage might be different. The financial aspects are covered in more detail in a later chapter. The actual length of time that insurance will pay for your care recipient to stay in the facility is determined by their progress, as evaluated by the therapists mostly. If your care recipient is participating in and making progress in therapy, Medicare will continue to pay up to the 100 days. But, they may plateau (stop making progress) before then. Medicare determines whether the gains being made are sufficient to justify the continued payment on a weekly basis. There can also be medical factors, and therefore a doctor is also involved, but they usually don't get heavily involved unless there is an insurance denial that they feel can justifiably be appealed. Remember that in a SNF the doctor is not likely to visit daily, so if there are

---

[13] medicare.gov/care-compare/

medical concerns you may need to request a meeting. Nonetheless, you should be prepared that once Medicare determines a denial you will have a short notice that the stay in the facility is over. You will usually only receive a day or two advance notice of discharge, and if you do not take your care recipient out of the facility at that time they will start charging them privately.

Remember when I said that a stay in the hospital is no fun? Well, a stay in a nursing and rehabilitation center is no walk in the park either! Your care recipient is likely to request to go home much sooner than it is recommended by their medical professionals. Consistent with the advice I gave regarding hospitalizations, bear in mind all of the same advice I gave about "AMA" discharges as it applies here as well. Encourage your care recipient to follow their advice and stay in the facility as long as is recommended. Make the effort to keep them as comfortable as possible by bringing the comforts of home to them, such as their bed spread, family photos, or a favorite coffee mug. Also keep in mind that a "spoonful of sugar" really does make the medicine go down, so you may want to sweeten the deal by planning an activity or reward for when they are released. You might set a goal tied to this incentive, such as "once you can walk 100 feet unassisted, we will be able to go to the beach for the weekend". But in all honesty, the best approach with a care recipient who adamantly wants to leave the nursing facility too soon is the ultimatum. Reminding your care recipient that the stronger and healthier they get in the facility, the more successful they will be in the home setting and able to avoid long term care placement is a good motivator for most. It certainly won't be fun but encourage them that the significant physical gains they will receive will make it worth it.

In addition to convincing your care recipient it is best for them to stay put, it is also entirely likely you will need to advocate at some point during this process (and possibly multiple times). Now, it is important to recognize that when your care recipient is going to a skilled nursing facility for short term rehabilitation, this is a completely different thing from long term care placement. As I mentioned, most provide both levels of care. These are two completely different experiences even if provided in the same physical building. In a later chapter I will talk more about skilled nursing facilities from a long term care aspect. Regardless of whether your care recipient will be spending time in a skilled nursing facility short term or long term, I always gave the families of my new residents in the nursing facility the same advice. Show up! Visit as often as possible and get to know the staff. You catch more bees with honey and a simple gesture of appreciation for the caring staff will go a long way in establishing a rapport. The staff will appreciate your involvement and when you have a request or concern, you will get much better cooperation from them if they have an existing positive relationship with you.

It is also important to know who the long-term care ombudsman is in your area. This is the government agency's representative responsible for advocating on a community level for residents who reside in these types of facilities, both short term and long term. Separate from the licensing and regulatory bodies, the LTCO is a third-party advocate that family members and caregivers can look to for education, support, and guidance regarding their care recipient's care and treatment in a facility. Their primary function is to preserve and protect resident rights and ensure quality of care. Remember one of the two S's in the GUESS acronym- seek support. Knowing who the long term care ombudsman is in your locale and how to reach them will go a long way in the support department!

I want to close out this section with words of encouragement. Having your care recipient go to a facility for rehabilitation for any length of time after a hospitalization can be frightening. The information I gave you in this section is intended to keep your expectations realistic and dispel common myths, but I also want to emphasize to you that I recommend doing it because it is truly worth it. If you are planning ahead and have the luxury of time, it can be helpful to tour and be knowledgeable about the facilities in your area ahead of the time of need, so that your care recipient can select the ones they would be most willing to go to. Having some control over the choice and knowing what to expect makes it a pill much easier to swallow.

Take heart, most of these facilities have good programs and competent, caring people who truly want to help older adults get better. Yes, staffing ratios are undoubtedly a challenge, but you are likely to encounter phenomenal caregivers that will go above and beyond to take excellent care of your care recipient. Most people have skewed ideas of nursing facilities based on stories they heard in the news or from third parties. While it is of course important to be aware of and report mistreatment or substandard care, don't go into it with the assumption that you will encounter those things. They are rare and often embellished. You should always follow your gut about these things, remain observant, and do not ignore any instances of abuse. But, it is more likely than not that you will have a good experience and find that you and the staff share mutual concern over quality for your care recipient.

MEDICAL BILLS

One final recommendation I have about navigating the medical system is to be vigilant about medical bills. Medical billing and coding is one of the most confusing "languages" on the planet. It will serve you well to keep all bills, statements, receipts and Explanation of Benefits (EOBs) and good documentation of all conversations with insurance companies and providers. You should review all bills and reconcile with the EOBs, to watch for errors. Errors happen, more frequently than you might expect.

If you receive a bill and it seems inaccurate, don't hesitate to call and question it. If the bill is too vague, ask for an itemized bill that is clearer on what you are being charged for. When you speak to a billing representative, keep records of who you spoke to and what they told you. Always call with a concern promptly, so that you do not end up in a past due status or collections situation simply because you don't know what you owe.

Furthermore, many providers will send two bills, one before insurance has made its payments and adjustments and one after. This is a very confusing practice. Don't pay anything you aren't required to until after you have received the bill that shows what your insurance has already paid.

If you find yourself experiencing problems with medical billing above and beyond what you can handle, it might make sense to hire a Medical Billing Specialist. You can search for professionals who provide this type of service via the Alliance of Claims Assistance Professionals. You can also contact the Patient Advocate Foundation, a nonprofit that offers free advice and assistance to people who need help with medical bills and insurance company appeals.[14]

---

[14] patientadvocate.org

CARING FOR DEMENTIA

"People will forget what you said, people will forget what you did, but people will never forget how you made them feel."
-Maya Angelou

One of the most common and significantly debilitating illnesses that affects older adults is dementia. So much so that caring for dementia is entirely worthy of its own publications, and there have been many fantastic texts written on the subject. I will reference some of them in the index. Because dementia is both so common and so difficult to manage, it is the only diagnosis I am going to go into in any detail about in this book. I also felt that while it is a medical diagnosis, it deserved to stand apart from the rest of the medical chapter. If your care recipient does not have dementia, feel free to move on to chapter three. However, I feel every caregiver should at least have a basic knowledge of dementia and what is involved with caring for someone living with it because it so frequently crops up and oftentimes goes unrecognized for quite some time. I intend to keep my overview of dementia high-level and provide some suggestions for overcoming the added challenges dementia presents in the journey of caregiving.

First, let's review the difference between Alzheimer's and dementia. The terms are often used interchangeably, but dementia is more precisely an umbrella term that encompasses many different types of cognitive impairments. While you may see it in your care recipient's medical chart, dementia is not a diagnosis in and of itself. Truth be told, when someone receives a diagnosis of "dementia", what they are really being diagnosed with is a set of symptoms that affect memory and cognitive functioning.

It is also important to recognize that dementia is not a normal part of aging. I cannot tell you how many times I have heard phrases along the lines of "mom didn't have Alzheimer's, she just had normal old age dementia". There is no such thing. Dementia is common, but it is not normal. It is true that most people, regardless of age, will experience memory lapses or forgetfulness. Forgetting the occasional person's name or the day of the week is "normal", as long as you can do the mental work and come to an answer at some point. Memory loss that is associated with dementia is more than these examples. Dementia is disruptive to day-to-day functions, making it hard for one to plan, make decisions, problem solve and remain oriented to person, place and time.

Furthermore, dementia can be "acute" – meaning that it affects a person for a limited amount of time but can be potentially treated and resolved. This type of dementia can also be referred to as delirium in medical terms. However, dementia can also be chronic, meaning that it is a progressive illness that won't go away. I will be focusing on management of chronic dementias, and specifically Alzheimer's in this text, but bear in mind it is important if you suspect your care recipient has dementia to ensure that acute causes are ruled out first. There is a mnemonic device that I have seen several different versions of in the nursing community throughout my time in this field. The device itself is very easy to remember because it is the word – DEMENTIA. However, what each letter stands for fluctuates in different versions I have seen. The following is the most common version:[15]

D- Drugs (medication side effects or interactions)

E- Eyes & Ears (problems with hearing and eyesight)

M- Metabolic & Endocrine (disorders of these systems)

E- Emotional Turmoil (such as depression)

N- Nutrition/Hydration (malnourishment)

T- Trauma (such as a concussion)

I- Infection (such as a urinary tract infection)

A- Alcohol (it is important to note that long term effects of alcohol can cause chronic dementia)

In addition to the conditions referenced in the above list, delirium can

---

[15] Mnemonic for Assessing DEMENTIA June 5, 2017 by Lane Therrell FNP, MSN, RN, MSN, RN, NP

also be caused by other things such as effects of anesthesia, hydrocephalus, environmental changes, poisoning/toxicity, insomnia, exacerbation of mental illness and more. Therefore, it is imperative to have a full medical workup to determine if any of these causes are applicable to your care recipient's situation before jumping to the conclusion of Alzheimer's or any other chronic dementia.

Once the aforenamed causes have been ruled out, you will likely be headed towards a diagnosis of Alzheimer's or some other chronic dementia disease. Of the chronic dementia diseases, Alzheimer's disease is the most common and widely known type. But, not all chronic dementia is Alzheimer's disease. There are many other types of chronic dementia, including Vascular dementia, dementia with Lewy bodies, Frontotemporal dementia (includes ALS), Creutzfeldt-Jakob's disease, Parkinson's dementia and dementia related to Huntington's disease. Symptoms, pathology, and progression of each of these diseases depend heavily on the part of the brain that is affected by them.

Alzheimer's disease is a neurodegenerative disorder that causes progressive and irreversible loss of neurons and brain functioning. The exact causes are not certain, but scientists have identified that amyloid plaques and neurofibrillary tangles exist in the brains of patients with Alzheimer's. These plaques and tangles interfere with communication between brain cells. It is also known that the brains of patients with Alzheimer's shrink and/or deteriorate, particularly in the rear of the brain. Alzheimer's disease is not reversible and there is no cure. Alzheimer's causes a loss of executive functioning that makes it very difficult to manage daily tasks. Executive functioning refers to high level thinking, the type of mental processing that allows us to learn, adapt to our environment, and carry out necessary tasks.

There are more than ten genes that have been linked to increased likelihood that you will develop Alzheimer's disease if they are present. The most common is called apolipoprotein E (APOE).[16] There are several different types of APOE. Having at least one will greatly increase your risk of developing Alzheimer's, but does not guarantee it.

Unfortunately, you can't do anything about genetic risk factors. There are

[16] NIH RESEARCH MATTERS March 16, 2021 Study reveals how APOE4 gene may increase risk for dementia by Erin Bryant

however risk factors that you can do something about and they are lifestyle related. People who live a healthy lifestyle, particularly after their mid-life point, are less likely to develop Alzheimer's disease. Not smoking, engaging in regular physical activity, maintaining a healthy weight, and eating a healthy primarily plant-based diet can go a long way in reducing the risk of developing all types of dementia, not to mention other chronic illnesses.

In the early stages, it might be hard to identify whether memory problems are "normal", or a sign of something worse. If you have this concern, you may want to start with the guide I put together for this chapter on the signs and symptoms of dementia. Next, it is worth having an evaluation done by a physician to determine if Alzheimer's is a concern. Addressing new behaviors with a family doctor is a good first step. Unless one goes through very specific cognitive and neuropsychological testing, the exact diagnosis of Alzheimer's disease cannot technically be given. Therefore, if the primary physician feels the symptoms are concerning enough to warrant it, he or she may refer you to a neurologist (doctors who specialize in neurocognitive disorders) for further workup to either rule out or diagnose a specific type of dementia. The general path to a diagnosis consists of some initial testing such as urine, liver, thyroid, potassium levels, and Vitamin D, B6 and B12 levels. After that, cognitive and neuropsychological testing may be performed, followed by more advanced testing such as MRIs, PET or CAT scans.

STAGES OF ALZHEIMER'S

Caregivers often struggle with understanding exactly how far along in the disease process their care recipient is. This is likely because the stages are not clearly defined. It is also complicated by the fact that the progression varies from person to person. Some people may progress very quickly through certain stages and seemingly not experience them at all. Others might linger in a particular stage for much longer than expected.

Broadly speaking there are three stages of Alzheimer's Disease: mild (early), moderate (mid) and severe (late). However, clinically Alzheimer's Disease has been broken down into seven stages by Dr. Barry Reisberg of New York University. This is the model that is recognized by the Alzheimer's Association.[17]

Stage 1 is the No Impairment stage. In this stage there is no evidence of dementia. The patient will be functioning normally.

Stage 2-3 are the mild (early) stages. More than half of persons over the age of 65 report concerns with cognitive difficulties including forgetfulness and difficulty concentrating. It can be very hard to tell if these symptoms are pre-dementia or normal aging. These individuals may start to struggle with managing tasks that are normally easy for them, such as balancing a checkbook. It also becomes harder for them to learn new things. However, they are usually still able to recognize their deficits, which can start to cause anxiety.

By the time the person living with Alzheimer's reaches stage 3, their deficits may become more pronounced. For example, you may arrive at your mother's home to take her to a doctor's appointment, and she is dressed for the wrong season. Friends and loved ones who have regular contact with the individual will likely notice the beginnings of short term memory loss, but savvier individuals may continue to be able to hide most of their deficits from others. This is because they show no obvious memory impairments outwardly. Oftentimes, people in this stage will begin to socially withdraw which is a defense mechanism. The less likely they interact with other people, the less likely their cognitive deficits will be noticed.

At this point, physicians are usually able to make an accurate diagnosis. Your care recipient may need adjustments to be made to function in an independent living environment.

Stage 4 is the beginning of the mid (moderate) stage. There will likely be a notable decline in ability to manage daily activities. They may begin to exhibit disorientation to time and place, and not be able to recognize what is going on in the environment around them. The symptoms are severe enough to be extremely disruptive to day to day life and they should no longer be living independently without assistance as they will not be able to reliably recognize potential harm to themselves or others.

---

[17] https://alzheimersdisease.net/reisbergs-stages

Stages 5-7 are the transition from moderate and then to severe. From this point forward, it becomes murkier for caregivers and physicians alike in pinpointing exactly what stage a patient is in. When the patient has reached Stage 5, cognitive deficits are much more obvious and frequent. They generally are still able to follow simple commands and communicate, but they are completely unable to manage their own personal care sufficiently. They will require much more physical assistance and rely heavily on others to complete day to day tasks for them. Mobility becomes severely compromised and communication becomes extremely difficult.

By stage 7, the brain becomes so deteriorated that basic reflexes such as swallowing become impossible and the body just shuts down. They will no longer recognize being hungry or thirsty. The brain deterioration will lead to other organs in the body eventually shutting down. This is what ultimately causes death in patients with Alzheimer's if they do not die from another ailment in the meantime.

DEMENTIA MEDICATIONS

We discussed medication management earlier as being an area that causes a lot of difficulty for caregivers. Adding to the confusion for people in dealing with dementia is the medications used to "treat" it. First, I want to be clear that there are no medications or treatments currently on the market that can cure Alzheimer's. However, the clinical research being done in this area is vast, and the landscape is changing frequently.

Currently, there are only a handful of FDA approved medications available, which fall into two categories. The first are Cholinesterase inhibitors, which are medications used for mild to moderate stages of dementia and may help manage the symptoms of Alzheimer's and other dementias. The second are Glumate regulators, which are medications used for moderate to severe dementia that may help slow down the progression of cognitive decline.

The medications in both categories are very commonly prescribed. However, there is usually very little education provided to the patient and caregiver about the medications. It can be very difficult to determine just how much, if at all, any of these drugs are helping. Most of the time it seems they are prescribed and then continued to be used indefinitely, whether helpful or not. In some cases, the side effects may not be worth the benefits. Therefore I once again recommend using the symptom and activity log to monitor how your care recipient is doing and communicate any noticeable side effects to their physician. Unless it is brought to a physician's attention, they are not likely to bring this up and many people remain on these drugs for years after they have stopped providing any benefit to the patient.

There was a new drug approved by the FDA in the United States in 2021, Aducanumab which is an anti-amyloid antibody treatment administered by IV infusion.[18] It works by targeting the protein fragments that form in the brain and turn into the plaques and tangles I talked about earlier. This drug's approval was controversial however and Medicare's coverage of the drug is limited.

It is important to be aware that it is very common to see the use of antipsychotic medications to manage behavioral symptoms associated with Alzheimer's and other dementias. Because antipsychotic medications are for treating psychiatric illnesses such as schizophrenia, bipolar and others, the use of them to treat dementia patients is considered off-label. Essentially, these medications do very little to treat the disease and are used merely to induce a calming effect. The over-use of these medications to calm a patient with dementia can be very dangerous for multiple reasons.

Using non-pharmacological interventions is the best way to manage the behaviors associated with Alzheimer's. As I mentioned, I am not going to go into detail about Alzheimer's and other dementias. However, because dementia is such a common illness and challenge for caregivers, and the medications and treatments currently available are minimal, I would be remiss to not touch on some of the most common behaviors and provide some strategies to manage them. Therefore, the next section will outline some of those.

I will wrap up this section by mentioning that there will at times be "fad" over the counter or "natural" treatments for dementia that you may become aware of.

---

[18] https://www.alz.org/alzheimers-dementia/treatments/aducanumab

For example, there was quite a bit of talk in mainstream media around ten years ago about coconut oil possibly being able to "treat" or "prevent" Alzheimer's. While it may be attractive to try fads like this, because you may think "how can it hurt?"- the fact is, it can hurt. You should never implement an over the counter or "natural" supplement or treatment into your care recipient's regimen without consulting their physician and discussing the possible side effects or interactions with medications they are currently taking.

MANAGING DEMENTIA BEHAVIORS

When living with a diagnosis of dementia, your care recipient is dealing with one of the most frightening and challenging experiences of their lives. It is easy, especially in the earlier stages, to think they are just being "stubborn", "irrational" or "difficult". The truth is, they are struggling. They are fearful. They may be in denial. Furthermore, they may begin to exhibit unpredictable, erratic and sometimes aggressive behaviors. This is usually the most alarming thing for caregivers to experience.

Unfortunately, resources for older adults who are experiencing mental illnesses are slim. I will not delve into this topic in detail but what I will state is that it is important to remember that dementia is not a mental illness and should not be treated as such. It is possible that an older adult may be experiencing both an exacerbation of underlying mental illness as well as dementia, and this possibility should not be ignored in those who have a history of mental illness. If you suspect this to be the case, be sure to bring it up with your care recipient's PCP or primary psychologist for guidance.

My most valuable piece of advice when it comes to managing dementia behaviors is never to argue with your care recipient. Instead, try to find common ground. They are living in an alternate reality that is very real to them while it is unknown to you. Do your best to recognize their reality and find a way to connect with them that involves understanding and patience, rather than trying to re-orient them to your reality. The resources for this chapter include a guide on dementia communication that will outline useful tips when caring for someone with dementia. Additionally, the following section will outline some of the most common behaviors people with Alzheimer's exhibit, and some strategies to manage them.

REPETITIVE QUESTIONING

Alzheimer's disease and other dementias cause problems with short-term memory. This can lead to the person with dementia repeating themselves or asking the same question over and over again. Your care recipient isn't doing it on purpose; they truly have no memory of asking you the first or fiftieth time. But even though unintentional, it can be annoying to some caregivers. That's why it's important to understand the underlying reasons for it, and use techniques that can help ease the line of questioning before you reach your limit.

People with dementia often exhibit repetitive questioning when something is bothering them, they are fearful or anxious. They are often confused so they ask questions to help reassure or orient themselves. They may not know why they are where they are or what is coming next and that gives them anxiety. Pacing is also something frequently observed in persons with dementia.

When your care recipient starts to exhibit this behavior, first try to rule out things that might be giving them anxiety. Calmly respond to their repetitive question, but then perhaps consider whether changing the setting will be helpful, or reducing stimuli like television, or offering a snack to see if they are hungry or a sweater to see if they are cold. In some cases introducing something calming like soft music or a simple activity can be helpful. This is known as redirection. For example if your care recipient keeps asking if it is dinner time, but you just had lunch and you know they aren't hungry, suggest they fold laundry or sort some magazines with you.

If the repetitive questioning continues, it is easiest to keep your answers simple and consistent. This will prevent confusion and alleviate some of your care recipient's anxiety. When your answer is too complex, it can make them more confused and fearful. Remaining clear and concise will be beneficial for both of you.

Another strategy that works well for some caregivers in combating this type

---

[19] vfvalidation.org

of behavior is called Validation therapy, a type of therapy created by Naomi Feil between 1963 and 1980. You can learn more about her and her methods by following the link at the footnote below.[19] Validation therapy involves acknowledging the person living with dementia's feelings and meeting them where they are. If your care recipient is distraught that his or her deceased spouse is not there, it may be helpful to acknowledge that they miss them, and then ask them about a happy experience they had together. For example, you could try something like "I am sure you miss dad a lot. Tell me about your and dad's wedding." There are mixed reviews on validation therapy. Personally, I have seen it work extremely well for some and not so well for others. Overall, one of the most positive aspects of it from my perspective is that it slows us down and reminds us to think of how our care recipient is feeling, and not just focus on our own frustration or impatience.

UNWARRANTED SUSPICIONS

Sometimes people living with Alzheimer's disease and other dementias can become suspicious of their surroundings and other people. Often this is because they are misinterpreting things they see or hear. They are struggling to understand the environment around them, and therefore suspicion comes naturally. It is important not to respond in a defensive manner if your care recipient accuses you of an action that you didn't perform. You may be taken aback, but don't take it personally. It is important to remember that it is their disease telling them to be suspicious of you.

I have experienced situations where adult children are accused of theft, spouses are accused of cheating, and the list goes on. This can be very surprising and hurtful to the person being accused. If the person with dementia thinks something of theirs has been lost or stolen, a tactic that can be used is that you "borrowed" it or took it to the shop for repair, cleaning, etc., and that you will return with the item later. Once I had a family moving their mother into the memory care facility where I worked. Their mother wore a lot of jewelry, mostly costume, every day. Her daughter was very concerned about losing her wedding ring that was worth tens of thousands of dollars, and was a cherished reminder of her late husband. The day of the move in, the daughter took the ring and told her mother that she was going to get it cleaned and bring it back. Her mother hesitantly agreed. However, after her daughter left she did not remember that she told her she was taking it to be cleaned. Naturally, she was suspicious of the staff, continually looking for it and accusing the nurses of stealing it. She was constantly upset and angry about her wedding ring being missing. Her daughter was not willing to bring it back and leave it with her mother at the facility. Therefore, we came up with an alternative. The daughter was able to purchase a piece of costume jewelry that was similar enough to the wedding ring for her mother to wear without knowing the difference. The faux ring satisfied her and alleviated the problem.

If you find yourself in a situation such as this, stay calm, let your care recipient express their concern, and then respond in a way that is calming and reassuring. Offer to help them resolve the situation, and do not argue with them. I am not saying you have to falsely admit to wrongdoing, but simply acknowledge their feelings and move on, perhaps utilizing the redirection techniques we discussed earlier.

AGGRESSION

Sometimes the person living with dementia will become so agitated, confused, or suspicious that it will result in aggression. Usually, this type of acting out is because he or she cannot express him or herself fully, causing deep frustration. Some other forms of dementia besides Alzheimer's, such as Frontotemporal dementia and Creutzfeldt-Jakob's disease, tend to have aggression as a more severe and common symptom, and they usually exhibit it much earlier in the disease progress.

Aggressive behaviors could be verbal such as yelling, or even physical such as hitting. The first step in managing these behaviors, much like managing repetitive behaviors, is to try and identify triggers or pain points and remove them. Pain is a common trigger in people with dementia. It is important to carefully examine the environment and make adaptations as necessary. If a specific situation or activity causes aggressive behavior, it is best to avoid that activity in the future. Using a calm tone, try to reassure them and use the redirection tactic to suggest a different activity.

Some people living with dementia will exhibit a 360-degree change in personality. Those who are generally sweet, kind and docile can become aggressive and nasty, which is offensive and heartbreaking to their families. On the other hand, I have had families tell me that their sweet and quiet family member used to be nasty before the illness influenced a personality change. Clearly, the latter of the two would be more pleasant to deal with but aggressive behaviors in dementia can often be managed with the right approach and compassion.

SLEEP DISTURBANCES

Another common behavior associated with Alzheimer's disease is day/night confusion and a phenomenon known as sundowning. Sundowning is when a patient with Alzheimer's experiences increased confusion late in the day or at night. This is more common in the mid to later stages of the illness, and can be an extremely exhausting behavior for both the caregiver and care recipient.

Consider first what might be causing the increased confusion or irritation at night. There may be a catalyst that your care recipient cannot express– the temperature of the room, needing to use the restroom, or an uncomfortable bed for example. Make sure any pain or underlying health conditions that could be interrupting sleep are addressed. For example, sleep apnea is common among older adults and can cause difficulty sleeping.

If you cannot identify a catalyst, consider the course of the day. Perhaps they are experiencing exhaustion from a particularly busy day. It seems counter-intuitive that after a busy day that your care recipient would not be able to sleep. However, if you've raised small children, you will know how common this is in little ones. The added stimulation can keep the brain active and cause insomnia. The same can be said for older adults.

It is never a good idea to immediately introduce a sleep-inducing medication to manage this behavior. The risks of such medications for elderly individuals, especially those who have dementia, are too high. Your care recipient could be at a higher risk of increased confusion and potential falls that can result in injury or even death. You may want to consider a natural remedy, such as melatonin.

However, you should always speak to your care recipient's physician before administering anything new, even natural or herbal. It is also important to review your care recipient's medications with their doctor to determine if insomnia is a common side effect of any of them. In some cases, you may be able to adjust the timing or certain medications to alleviate the nighttime side effects. It is also important to remove or limit the use of alcohol and caffeine, especially in the afternoon or evening as these substances can be extremely disruptive to sleep.

The safest approach to managing this symptom is to allow them to pace in a controlled environment and calmly try and prompt them back to sleep once every few minutes. There are some other strategies you can implement to help reduce the effects of sundowning without using medication. First, stick as close to a daily routine as you are able. The familiarity of a routine is comforting to your care recipient and keeps them calm. Introduce any changes gradually when possible. Performing the same tasks and actions in the same order every day can help your care recipient feel secure, and more calm and collected. Schedule changes can be extremely disruptive and agitating so it is best to avoid them as much as possible and when they are necessary to make them as slight or gradual as possible. Keep wake and sleep times consistent, and do the same things in order each time. Also, make sure your care recipient is getting enough exercise and not sleeping too much during the day. Finally, it may be beneficial to have the largest meal at noon instead of evening, so that heavy digestion is not still occurring during sleep.

Consider also the environment. Perhaps lighting may need to be adjusted. Regular daylight exposure is extremely helpful to keep day and night reversal at bay. Spending time outdoors is the best way to expose your care recipient to regular daylight. If that is not possible, fluorescent lamps that emit low level blueish-white light may mimic daylight and help regulate circadian rhythms. A night light may also help reduce confusion when your care recipient wakes at night in the dark. If your care recipient is accustomed to having television on at night, my next recommendation may be more of a challenge. Nonetheless, removing television from the bedroom can have a positive impact. One reason for this is also related to light. The intrusive lights (particularly blue light) from the television interfere with falling asleep and continue to disrupt sleep if left on. Another reason is that it can overstimulate the brain. Consider instead playing soft music to provide comfort.

WANDERING

One of the most hazardous behaviors an Alzheimer's patient can exhibit is wandering and exit seeking. More than half of Alzheimer's patients will exhibit this behavior as their disease progresses. For obvious reasons this can cause many safety concerns. Prioritizing your care recipient's safety is of utmost importance. Like other behaviors associated with dementia, you may be able to reduce wandering with redirection and reassurance. Often, they are looking to perform an old task or routine, such as going to work. Simply informing them that it is Saturday could eliminate the urge to seek exit.

There are many things you can do within the physical space to eliminate safety issues. Remove tripping hazards such as throw rugs, cords, and clutter. Keeping doors closed and putting gates at stairwells can also be helpful. Sometimes a sign or artwork on a door can help deter persons with dementia from opening and exiting. Painting or wallpapering a door the same as the walls surrounding it can also be effective.

People with dementia may also be at risk of mistaking hazardous items. Much like "baby-proofing" a home when there are little ones afoot, it can be a good idea to "dementia-proof" the home. Items like household cleaners, bleach, detergents, can be easily confused and result in terribly harmful situations. Lock up toxic products and replace everyday household products (especially hand soap, shampoo, conditioner, etc.) with non-toxic options. There are many brands that are kid-friendly and this will provide safe alternatives for the person living with dementia.

If exiting is a concern, install deadbolt or slide-bolt locks on exterior doors and other doors to areas in the home such as basement stairs or garages where your care recipient could easily be harmed. Sometimes it may be necessary to install more than one lock, and placing one higher up can be effective. Of course this would not be appropriate if your care recipient is alone at any time as they would not be able to exit safely in the event of an emergency.

There are also various devices that can alert you that your care recipient is trying to exit such as warning bells or wireless monitors. Also check with your local police department, as some have location device detection services such as Project Lifesaver that you can enroll in in case your care recipient does manage to exit undetected.

I am not saying by any stretch of the imagination that you never want to let your care recipient out of the house. Fresh air and sunshine can do wonders to help alleviate behaviors and promote overall wellness. Especially if your care recipient was a lover of the outdoors in their youth, participating in safe outdoor activities can be very beneficial. The concern would be going out alone or unattended. Of course you will also want to choose days when the weather and environment are conducive for an outing.

If wandering and exit seeking becomes an apparent symptom for your care recipient, it will no longer be safe to leave him or her alone. There are also other factors that can cause living at home to be a non-viable option long-term. In those cases, consider either moving your care recipient in with you, bringing in in-home caregivers, or looking into senior living. You may also want to consult a certified occupational therapist who is trained in the risks associated with Alzheimer's, or a CAPS certified home remodeler to come in and consult on changes that could be made to make the environment safer for your care recipient. We will discuss all of these options in detail in a later chapter.

You should also make others aware. Tell your care recipient's friends and neighbors that they have the disease and wandering may occur. Ask them to be on the lookout for them. People often tend to be ashamed or scared to let others know about their illness, but the more people know the more they can help and be vigilant regarding their safety. Alzheimer's is nothing to be ashamed of, and the trend is such that by 2050, a projected 13.8 million people will be living with it in the US alone.[20] Barring any medical breakthroughs to prevent or cure the disease, the push to inform, educate and support those living with it will be imperative.

---

[20] https://www.alzint.org/resource/world-alzheimer-report-2009/

Your care recipient may exhibit all, some, or none of the aforenamed behaviors, but not all people will respond the same to varying approaches, and even the same person may not respond the same way each time. You will need to engage in trial and error to determine what works best for you and your care recipient. The best thing anyone can do to help their care recipient with dementia is to keep them engaged, and provide reassurance and loving care. This can be challenging, frustrating even, particularly when communication becomes increasingly difficult. Especially in these times of great stress, it is important to remember that your care recipient is more than their disease.

I have a friend who lost her father who lived with dementia several years ago. She started a blog about the joys she found in experiencing dementia first-hand with her father.[21] Throughout their journey, she consistently met her father where he was on any given day and did not struggle to bring him back to her own reality. In doing so, she connected and reconnected with him beautifully time and again which would not have been possible if she were more rigid in her approach. You can continue to foster a relationship with your care recipient that encompasses dignity and joy if you keep it at the forefront.

You must learn to recognize that they are still the person you knew them to be, but their world is no longer the world they were familiar with. They may seem to be living in another dimension, but they can still feel very real emotions and personal connection. My Grandmother forgot who I was. At that point in her disease progression, In her mind she had reverted back to a point in her life when I did not exist. My father still existed in her mind, as a young, newly married man. And, because I looked so much like my mother when she was young, she thought I was her. Again, I knew nothing about Alzheimer's disease back then. But, I would not argue with my Grandmother when she called me my mother's name. I would smile, nod and hold her hand. It didn't matter to me that she thought I was someone else. That person she thought I was meant something to her, and that was all that mattered. Maya Angelou wasn't referring to dementia with her famous quote, but the relevance is spot on. They may

---

[21] joyindementia.com/home

not remember your name but they know the *feeling* that they get when in your presence. Your voice, touch, smile, and interactions mean something to them. Take heart in knowing they want to be with you, that your interactions bring them joy, and that is all that matters. Live in the moment, and enjoy the connections as you are able.

Life expectancy with Alzheimer's disease, like any other chronic illness, varies depending on many factors. It is also hard to put a time frame on it because each Alzheimer's patient progresses differently, and it is often undiagnosed until moderate stages. The more advanced age at which a person is diagnosed, the life expectancy is significantly lessened. The average life expectancy after diagnosis is seven to ten years but in some cases it can be as short as two to three years. I have also known people who have lived much longer than ten years with the disease. Nancy Reagan referred to Alzheimer's disease as "the long goodbye". What she meant by this is that Alzheimer's causes your care recipient to slip away from you slowly. You have no way of knowing how much time you have but make the most of the time you have remaining with them. Continue to nurture your relationship, because when they are gone it is those memories that you will cherish forever.

As your care recipient's dementia progresses, it may become very exhausting on your family and its resources. We will talk in more detail about the financial side later, but, even with unlimited financial resources, dementia is one of the most difficult illnesses to manage. Nancy's beloved Ronnie stated in his famous letter addressing the Nation about his disease: "Unfortunately, as Alzheimer's disease progresses, the family often bears a heavy burden. I only wish there was some way I could spare Nancy from this painful experience".[22] The President lived with Alzheimer's for nearly a decade after penning this letter (maybe longer as the year of his onset is commonly debated). A decade is a long time to care for someone with dementia, particularly in the home setting. You may reach a point that you can no longer do it alone. Here are some questions you can ask yourself to determine if it is the right time to bring in outside resources:

· Are the care needs of my care recipient becoming more than I can handle

---

[22] reaganlibrary.gov/reagans/ronald-reagan/reagans-letter-announcing-his-alzheimers-diagnosis

on my own?

- Am I struggling to keep up with my other commitments and responsibilities to care for my care recipient?

- Is it becoming unsafe for my care recipient to be left alone at home? If your care recipient is wandering and exit seeking, you can try utilizing a monitor and motion sensor. But if the wandering is frequent enough this can get very exhausting and dangerous.

- Is the physical or mental health of my care recipient or my own as a caregiver declining in our current care arrangement?

If the answer to any of these questions is yes, it is time to consider that placement in a senior living facility may be the best option. We will explore these different options in the next chapter.

UNDERSTANDING YOUR CARE RECIPIENT

This checklist outlines what you should know about your care recipient's medical condition and baseline. This will equip you to answer medical provider's questions and make care decisions.

Medical Information:
- Primary diagnoses
- Secondary diagnoses
- Primary care physician's name and phone number
- Specialists names and phone numbers
- Known Allergies
- Health History
  - Hospitalizations
  - Surgeries
  - Recent tests
- Blood type
- Family medical history
- Location of Medical Records
- End of Life Wishes
- DNR if applicable

Medication List*:
- Prescribed Medications
  - Prescriber info
  - For what diagnosis is is prescribed
  - Where is it filled (pharmacy)
  - Dose and frequency
  - Form (pill, liquid, injection)
  - Route
  - Record of side effects noticed
- Over the Counter Medications
- Vitamins and supplements

Have multiple copies of the medication list. Keep one with you so that you can reference it when needed.

CAREGIVING BOUNDARIES ASSESSMENT
(ADL AND IADL)

Use this checklist to assess your care recipient's ability to perform the task on their own. Additionally, assess your comfort level with assisting if needed.

IADLs Baseline (mark the ones your care recipient is able to do on their own):
- Driving
- Preparing meals
- Cleaning
- Shopping
- Managing Household finances
- Medication Management

IADLs I am comfortable (and able to) assisting with if needed:

Driving:	Yes__ No__
Preparing meals:	Yes__ No__
Cleaning:	Yes__ No__
Shopping:	Yes__ No__
Managing Household finances:	Yes__ No__
Medication Management:	Yes__ No__

ADLs Baseline (mark the ones your care recipient is able to do on their own).
- Bathing
- Dressing
- Brushing and flossing teeth
- Grooming (such as brushing hair and trimming nails)
- Eating (Feeding oneself)
- Toileting
- Ambulation (walking)

ADLs I am comfortable (and able to) assisting with if needed:

Bathing: Yes__ No__

Dressing: Yes__ No__

Brushing and flossing teeth: Yes__ No__

Grooming: Yes__ No__

Eating (Feeding): Yes__ No__

Toileting: Yes__ No__

Ambulation: Yes__ No__

SAMPLE CAREGIVER LOG

This guide includes recommended information to keep track of each day.

Medical:
- Blood pressure
- Weight
- Temperature
- Blood sugar if applicable (diabetic)
- Pulse oximetry if applicable (on supplemental oxygen)

Medications:
- What was taken, when, and how much.
- Include vitamins, supplements, and over the counter medications
- Record any side effects noted or reported

Nutrition and Hydration:
- What was eaten, when, and how much.
- How much fluid was consumed throughout the day.

Output:
- How many times urinated throughout the day
- How many bowel movements throughout the day
- Record any difficulties noted or reported with either

Sleep:
- When did they sleep, for how long?
- Was sleep interrupted at all?
- Include nap times and duration

Mental Health:
- Attitude/demeanor
  > Positive observances may include: Happy, excited, friendly, peaceful, joyful, etc.
  > Negative observances may include: Irritated, annoyed, impatient,

unhappy, tired etc
> At any point during the day did they seem depressed or anxious?
> Did they express feelings of hopelessness, worthlessness, or despair?
> Did they at any point become tearful for no apparent reason?
> Were there any apparent triggers if they exhibited any of the above?
- Behaviors (if anything out of the ordinary occurred):
  > How long did the behavior last?
  > Were there any apparent triggers for the behavior?

Activities:

- Calls and/or visits by friends, family and others:
  > Who visited, when, and for how long.
  > What occurred during the visit.
- Exercise
  > Record any physical exercise including type, frequency, duration.
  > If the exercise is part of a care plan ordered by a professional, be sure to make notes for the professional to review.
- Outings/Appointments
  > Doctor Appointments
  > Other
- Leisure activities
  > Take note of any leisure activities they participated in such as reading, journaling, art, or listening to music.

Incidents:

- Record any incidents such as a fall or other type of accident.
- If the incident resulted in injury, document the specifics of what the injury is. For example, for skin tears write down the size and shape of the skin tear. Record what first aid measures were taken, if any.
- Remember to call 911 or report to the Emergency room for any of the following:

- Chest pain
- Unconsciousness
- Signs of a stroke (slurred speech, drooping of the face)
- Difficulty breathing
- Severe nausea/vomiting/diarrhea
- Inability to have a bowel movement for 3 or more days
- Blood in stool
- Abnormal or increased confusion

You can use either a paper log or an electronic one to record your care recipient's daily routine and activities. Keeping good records will help you identify patterns and triggers of certain symptoms.

PREPARING FOR DOCTOR'S VISITS

This guide includes suggested questions you may want to be prepared with for your doctor's visit.*

- First, be sure to talk with your care recipient before the appointment and review the care log to determine any specific concerns you want to address during the appointment.
- Also remember to bring your current medication list to the appointment. Have multiple copies so the doctor can keep one.

Questions may include:

- Review vitals. Are there any concerns?
- Is there a concern/risk for any particular health conditions?
- How could current conditions affect health down the road?
- Is there any preventative care we should be doing?
- Understand the prescribed medications. Ask clarifying questions such as:
  - > If there are multiple medications for the same condition, why?
  - > Are all prescribed medications necessary? Can anything be discharged?
  - > Should any vitamins or supplements be added to our regimen?
  - > If medication management is becoming difficult, ask for help with structuring the daily medication regimen to make it easier.
- New medications or treatments:
  - > Why are you prescribing this medication or treatment?
  - > How does this medication, treatment or procedure work?
  - > How long will it be needed?
  - > When should improvement occur?
  - > Understand potential side effects and drug interactions.
- Discharged Medications:
  - > Ask for instructions for disposal of unused medications safely
- Are there any diet recommendations?
- Are there any current vaccine recommendations such as flu,

pneumonia, or shingles.
· Bring up any issues with sleep.
· Understand any tests or labs that are to be done.
· If you don't understand any of the doctor's instructions, ask for clarification. If you cannot read written instructions, ask the doctor to "translate" their handwriting. Be sure you have a good understanding of what they recommended and why.
· If there is a need, ask a recommendation for a specialist, physical therapy, nutritionist, etc
· Discuss end of life planning: Understanding advance directives and DNR status.
· When should we come back?
· Is there anything we should work on before next visit?

This list is not comprehensive and should be tailored for each visit.

HOSPITAL DISCHARGE CHECKLIST

Use this checklist to ensure that you are fully prepared for your care recipient's hospital discharge.

New Medical Diagnosis:
- Understand fully any new diagnosis, prognosis and treatment plan
  - › Ensure you have been given education about managing the new diagnosis both verbally and in writing that you can understand
- Know what symptoms should you be aware of or looking out for going forward
- Know if there are dietary restrictions or suggested changes for your care recipient's diet
- Know what follow up appointments are needed, and whether they have been scheduled

New/discontinued/changed prescriptions:
- Ensure you have been educated on the dosage, route, frequency, and possible side effects and interactions
- Ask if their insurance cover the medication and if not, ask about less expensive alternatives
- Ask for physical prescriptions

Safety, Services and Equipment
- Find out if your care recipient's functional status changed (refer to the ADL checklist)
- Find out if there are any physical accommodations they might need at home to be able to maneuver safely
- Ask if they will need any adaptive equipment or medical supplies, and if so, find out if those have been ordered or if you need to get them
- Ask what specific tasks you are going to be entrusted with as their caregiver (don't be afraid to speak up if you are uncomfortable)
- Ask for training for any task you may be uncomfortable or unfamiliar with

- Ask if there is a need for services such as home care and if so, find out if referrals been made for these services and get the contact information for the providers (remember – you should be given the opportunity to vet them yourself)

Post-Discharge:

- You should be provided with assistance making transportation arrangements if necessary
- Ensure that hospital records are going to be sent to your care recipient's Primary care physician
- Learn what you should do if you have any questions or concerns within the hours and immediate few days post-discharge
- If you are worried about your care recipient managing at home, voice your concerns and ask a case manager or discharge planner to help arrange alternative plans

DEMENTIA SIGNS AND SYMPTOMS

Use this guide to help you determine whether what you are observing is normal, or if it may be the early warning signs of dementia.*

- Losing Things and not being able to retrace steps
- Inability to learn new things and/or following basic directions
- Difficulty carrying through a conversation
- Difficulty starting and/or completing tasks
- Difficulty adjusting to changes in routine
- Getting lost on familiar trips
- Difficulty planning things (such as a meal or a trip)
- Difficulty focusing
- Emotional outbursts/extreme mood swings
- Trouble expressing oneself appropriately
- Trouble managing a personal schedule
- Exhibiting poor judgment and decision making (for example, not dressed appropriately for season or occasion)
- Forgetting important/significant dates
- Repetitive questions
- Difficulty identifying familiar objects
- Reduced ability to solve problems
- Social withdrawal
- Difficulty handling finances (when they normally were skilled at this)

If you are beginning to notice any of the signs on this list, you should seek a medical opinion to rule out other possible causes and discuss the possibility of cognitive decline.

DEMENTIA COMMUNICATION TIPS

This guide provides tips to help you communicate effectively with your care recipient about day to day tasks and their care.

- Remain patient and calm
- Approach from the front, and at their eye level
- Speak clearly and slowly; you may need to repeat yourself
- Smile and make eye contact
- Be as clear and direct as possible, particularly when you are asking them to do something
- Do not give multiple steps at once
- Try to avoid causing unnecessary confusion; use terms and phrases they will understand
- Use comforting physical touch when appropriate
- Ask simple yes and no questions
- Do not give too many options
- Give them ample time to think and reply
- You may need to reword or rephrase your question, for example, instead of asking them what they would like for dinner, offer a choice: "Would you like chicken or fish for dinner?"
- Don't correct or argue with them
- Look for clues; try and determine what they are trying to tell you based on the context and their body language- this may help alleviate frustration
- Provide reassurance to them, especially when they seem overly confused and anxious

Other helpful tips:

- Keep tasks and routines simple and consistent
- Keep the environment calm and soothing; free of distractions
- Focus on what they can do, not their deficits
- Using picture cards can be helpful, for example, you could have a card with the picture of food and show it when asking if they are hungry

NOTES

CHAPTER 3

*You may not control life's circumstances, but getting to be the author of
your life means getting to control what you do with them.*
-Atul Gawande, Being Mortal

AGING IN PLACE OR ASSISTED LIVING?

It is a well-known fact that most older adults want to
age at home, and understandably so. Home is where the heart
is. They are emotionally attached to their home, and it is where
they are most comfortable. They worked hard to pay for, build and
maintain that home for a long time. They may have raised their
family there; it is filled with memories and joy for them. There is
a reason Dorothy's words resonate —"there's no place like home."
Think back to your favorite vacation, no matter how luxurious or
exciting it was, was there not still some pleasure in returning to
the comfort of your own
home when it was over?
Most would say yes. We
are most comfortable and
overall happy where we
are most familiar.

Knowing this, you may face a difficult quandary as you may be wondering if home is the right place for them to remain as they age. You may have doubts about their safety, or the ability to keep the home maintained. Countless times I have heard "I promised my [care recipient] I would never put [them] in a nursing home". With this promise lurking in the back of their minds, they painstakingly make every decision regarding their care recipient's care, committed to maintaining their dignity and well being. While I understand the emotional aspect of it, there are many factors to consider in making the right decision.

To age in place, 83 percent of American aging adults live with others and rely on others for support.[23] As we discussed earlier, the loss of the ability to perform IADLs and ADLs makes it much more difficult for older adults to live independently. Bearing that in mind it shouldn't come as a surprise that based on a 2020 survey more than 65 million people are providing care for a chronically ill, disabled, or aged individual, spending an average of 20 hours per week each year providing care for their care recipient.[24] If you plan to keep your care recipient at home, you can expect there is a good chance you will end up in this boat.

Now don't take the aforementioned concern as my strict endorsement of senior living over aging in place. I happen to be a big proponent of aging in place as an option for older adults. While we were unable to make this dream a reality for my grandmother, I have seen many success stories of aging in place and I have seen very successful assisted living placements. What I will say is that aging in place involves more careful planning and has many more moving parts. You must take your care recipient's wishes and goals into consideration and as with any major decision, weigh the pros and cons of each before heading definitively one way or the other.

Perhaps the most important thing to keep in mind is that people are social creatures. Whether we are introverted or extroverted, we crave connection with others. In relation to Maslow's hierarchy we discussed earlier, I am talking about the third category of needs he describes in his pyramid – the one related to love and belonging. Humans must experience feelings of intimacy with other human beings. Without that, depression and feelings of worthlessness creep in. In our youth, we

[23] Where We Live, Where We Age: Trends in Home and Community Preferences by Joanne Binette, AARP Research, November 2021 Home and Community Preferences Survey
[24] NATIONAL ALLIANCE FOR CAREGIVING AND AARP PRESENT: CAREGIVING IN THE U.S. 2020: EXECUTIVE SUMMARY

have ample opportunity to experience love and belonging. We not only have the nuclear family in the home to provide these connections, but we also are more active in our communities through working, volunteering, religious and civic affiliations, hobbies and the like. But as we get older, the opportunities for connection with other humans become less accessible.

The next chapter goes further into the social aspects, but for now consider that access to human connection through which love and belonging can be actualized should be a primary factor in deciding where your care recipient should live as they age. Remember to keep Maslow's Hierarchy in mind as you weigh the options. Forthcoming in this chapter I will provide detail about both aging in place and senior living. I also provide a guide to help you in comparing aging in place vs. assisted living to get you started.

AGING IN PLACE CONSIDERATIONS

It is likely that your care recipient desires to "age in place", as most older adults do. You may be wondering how to help make this a reality for them. What needs to be considered when deciding if "aging in place" is a good option for your care recipient? The answer is a vast number of things that depend on the specific situation and circumstances. As this section unfolds, I will explore some of those factors and how they may affect your care recipient's ability to remain independent over time.

HOME SAFETY

First and foremost, the safety and functional aspects of the home environment must be assessed. Many older adults have lived in one place for a long time. This means that as they have aged, so has their home. This can lend itself to some serious safety concerns, most of which will need to be addressed by a professional. However, remember what the "E" stands for in GUESS – educate yourself on some of the immediate actions you can take that will make a considerable positive impact on home safety.

The free checklist the CDC provides is a good place to start.[25] This checklist

---

[25] cdc.gov/steadi/pdf/check_for_safety_brochure-a.pdf

will guide you on the most common hazards to address and provide some simple steps you can take to make the home environment safer. You may also want to arrange for a home visit to be done by an Occupational Therapist and/or an Aging in Place Specialist. They will evaluate the environment and provide recommendations for improvements that can be made. This will help ensure that your care recipient will be in the optimal environment to perform their ADLs and IADLs as safely as possible in their home.

A primary safety concern for older adults is falling. As we age, the harder the impact our body takes from a fall, and the more likely we are to experience injury. The resulting injuries may be minor such as skin tears or bruising, but they can also be much worse. According to the CDC, one in five falls causes a serious injury, such as broken bones or even traumatic brain injuries.[26] What's even more frightening is that falls can be fatal to the elderly, as one of the top five causes of injury-related death in persons over the age of 65.[27] This makes adjusting the environment to prevent falls or other accidents a top priority. Falls are accidents, and many are avoidable by taking certain actions to decrease risks in the home setting. There are three primary preventative measures you can take.

The first is adding safety features that do not require extensive reconstruction. Specialized equipment such as handrails, grab bars and raised toilet seats can be installed to make things safer. Ideally, the home where your care recipient wants to remain should be set up for one-floor living, with access to a full bathroom that either is or can be modified for accessibility. If that is not possible, a chair lift is a great option to reduce the potential for falls on stairs.

By and large the riskiest room of the home for older adults is the bathroom. One might suspect the kitchen, which of course houses a number of potential hazards as well. However, most falls occur in the bathroom. One easy way to make trips to the bathroom safer is to ensure that the path is well lit for middle of the night trips. Sometimes you will hear it advised to remove all bath mats. I don't suggest removing them completely, as a wet floor is certainly more

---

[26] cdc.gov/falls/facts.html
[27] cdc.gov/injury/wisqars/index.html

hazardous than a bath mat, but it is a good idea to use non-slip mats, with a low pile surface, so as to ensure they are less of a tripping hazard. If your care recipient wears bedroom slippers, make sure they are non-slip and have a back to them.

A walk-in shower with a handheld showerhead is ideal along with the use of a shower stool or chair. If your care recipient does not have a walk-in shower and the expense of adding one is too great, a less expensive option is getting a tub bench that makes getting in the tub easier. These benches are longer and do not fit entirely inside the tub, but instead, they extend over the edge to the outside so that a person can sit on the outside and carefully slide into the tub while sitting on a stable surface. It is also prudent to have grab bars near both the tub and the toilet. Grab bars are a relatively inexpensive and easy change to make that can be truly life-saving. You don't necessarily have to make permanent changes. Instead, you could install grab bars that can be easily removed upon sale of the home. You can also use a raised toilet seat to make getting on and off the commode a much safer activity. Many raised toilet seats also include handlebars, so you can eliminate the need for installing them on the wall next to the toilet.

You should also avoid storing items on high shelves where a step stool would have to be used for access. Older adults should not use step stools as they have decreased balance and mobility and this could be a prime opportunity for a detrimental fall. Instead, store heavy items at waist level, and ensure the lighting in storage areas is sufficient.

A second way to present falls is to ensure your care recipient is maintaining a strong and healthy body through physical exercise. Some falls happen simply because of risk factors as we age such as poor vision, decreased balance, muscle weakness, and slower reflexes. But exercise will increase balance, coordination and strength which will aid in both avoiding falls and reducing the risk of injury in the event of a fall. If your care recipient has deficits in this area, one resource that can be utilized is physical therapy. Physical therapy (and occupational therapy, too) has numerous benefits for older adults. For example, when your care recipient is debilitated and weak from illness or injury, physical therapy can help restore function, improve mobility, increase balance and coordination, and decrease pain.

When treating an older adult, physical therapists may use a combination of techniques including physical exercise such as strength training, stretching and walking, and sometimes other therapies to decrease pain and swelling such as massage, hydrotherapy, heat and cold therapy, ultrasound or electrical stimulation. They will develop a plan specific to the patient's condition and goals.

Education is a critical part of the process when working with a physical therapist. Safety is always at the forefront, therefore patients are given knowledge to protect themselves from injury or re-injury while exercising, and how to move about within their environment in a safe manner. Furthermore, I strongly encourage you to be mindful not to discourage your care recipient from remaining active in the pursuit of safety. This can be difficult to do. As a caregiver, our nature is to step in and do for someone who we view as vulnerable or frail. We should however be careful not to overdo it. If we do everything for our care recipient, they will begin to lose their independence more quickly than if they do as much as possible for themselves.

Finally, consider the use of a personal emergency fall device. In the event of a fall, summoning help immediately can be life-saving. I have heard numerous horror stories about falls that left their victim lying on the floor. My friend Crystel who wrote the foreword to this book is a good example. Her grandmother fell in the bathroom and was unattended for days. Thankfully, she did not suffer any broken bones. One of my home care clients was not so lucky. She fell while getting out of the tub and broke her fibula, but was on the floor for two days waiting for help to arrive. Like Crystel's grandmother, she became dehydrated and malnourished. I will never forget the look on her nephew's face as he told me the story. To imagine a frail elderly person lying on the floor, injured and unable to get up is torturous. A personal emergency device can make all the difference.

Many people are familiar with the alert button lanyards, which are a great option. However, some older adults are opposed to wearing the alert button lanyards, as they are unsightly and can be a nuisance, and they do have their limitations. There is a wide variety of devices with various features, service options and prices available on the market. To help you narrow down your search, you should first decide if you want a home-based or mobile option. If your care recipient is not homebound, a mobile option can enable them to call for help even when they are out, as they generally work over cell networks and have GPS technology. You should also consider whether the system is monitored and in what way. Some systems connect with a 24/7 call center that can dispatch emergency help if needed. Others will dial any number you program such as a caregiver or family member. These are of course not fail safe, but they do provide a comforting layer of security and protection. Pricing will vary depending on the services and features you opt for. Other options can include using technology that isn't specifically designed as a personal emergency alert but can function similarly such as smart watches, or even a digital home assistant.

EMERGENCY PLANNING

It is always a good idea to plan for emergencies, particularly for vulnerable older or disabled adults who may face additional hurdles due to physical and medical frailty. It is important to remember that disasters can happen at any time to anyone no matter where you live. It is always prudent to follow the Boy Scout motto of "be prepared". By planning ahead you can avoid situations where your care recipient is trapped without essential items.

First, put together an emergency kit consisting of essential items that will make evacuation or isolation during an emergency easier. Make sure your kit is packed in such a way that it can be easily grabbed and taken along in an evacuation. I have put together a guide for constructing this kit.

Additionally, Make a list of important contacts for home utilities and other emergency contacts. This can be helpful to you, your care recipient and other members of your advocacy team alike. If possible, include at least one non-local emergency contact. Sometimes it will be easier to reach someone who lives out of the area immediately following a natural disaster or other emergency.

Make sure your care recipient knows the safest places within the home in case they need to shelter during extreme weather events. Should they need to evacuate, plan how and where they should go. Inquire into the emergency plans and procedures that exist in their community. Investigate the community's response and evacuation and make arrangements for transportation if they cannot transport themselves. If they receive in-home care, speak with the agency's management to find out how they can help with your plan. In fact, in many states this is a requirement of the regulations that govern in-home care agencies. Once a plan is in place, be sure to share it with your family, friends and caregivers, and practice it at least twice a year. A well mapped out plan can go a long way.

Fire safety is also important to have a plan for. Avoid using appliances that could easily be turned on by accident, such as stovetops with knobs that protrude and could be bumped. In the event of a fire, an older or disabled person may have a slower reaction time to putting out the fire or getting to safety. It is also crucial to test smoke detectors monthly, and replace batteries every year. You may want to also investigate automatic shut-off devices. They can be costly but the peace-of-mind is priceless.

GEOGRAPHICAL CONSIDERATIONS

Another important factor when it comes to aging in place is the community or neighborhood in which your care recipient lives. If they live in a rural area, aging in place can prove to be much more difficult to do. There are many reasons for this. First, people living in rural areas tend to have larger homes and plots of land, which may become harder to keep up with later in life. Furthermore, while an older adult who lives in a rural community may feel they have more support, the reality is usually that their friends and neighbors are aging with them. They may be able to look after one another to an extent, but it is likely they will begin to experience challenges with aging along the same timelines.

There are also less public resources available in rural communities. Being far away from a hospital and medical services can be extremely challenging for older adults. It is true that telehealth has made significant advances in recent years. But, many older adults have a hard time using such technology, and being further from an emergency center when you have a truly life threatening emergency is very problematic. It is also harder for home health and other medical support companies to provide services and staff to rural areas. This can result in coverage gaps and missed appointments.

Finally, there is an increased risk of isolation of older adults living in rural areas. There is not likely to be public transportation options so as the older adult becomes unable to drive, they will face challenges with being able to leave home at all. We will discuss some of the risks of this isolation more in the next chapter.

MULTI-GENERATIONAL LIVING

When your care recipient loses their ability to live on their own, you may consider moving them into your home to live. You may feel that this is simply the right thing to do, especially if they cared for you as a child when you could not take care of yourself. But, there are several things that you should consider first to determine if it is the right fit, and to ensure that you approach it in the right way.

The first consideration is whether your home is physically conducive to multigenerational living. Multigenerational living can be very difficult if there is not enough private space for each person to feel comfortable. You may be able to make some modifications to accommodate, such as converting a garage or basement into an in-law suite. But if extensive remodeling is needed it may not make good financial sense. And, as we discussed earlier, you will need to consider the same safety concerns in your home as you would their own. A basement in-law suite for example isn't necessarily the safest option. In this arrangement, your care recipient will have to come up the stairs to the main level living areas, which is just as unsafe as going up to their bedroom.

If you can easily put in a stair lift, this might be a solution, but the ability of your care recipient to get out safely in an emergency is still going to be hampered by slowness. Furthermore, I have frequently seen families convert or build a separate building on their property (perhaps a detached garage for example). This works well while the care recipient is still independent. However, as their care needs increase this becomes less desirable. I had a client with my home care agency that had an in-law suite that was separated from the main home by a breezeway. The care recipient had dementia, and as it progressed, she was unsafe to be in the separated area alone. The family was growing tired of checking on her so frequently to ensure her safety that they hired our agency for around the clock care. This was a very expensive solution and unfortunate considering she was so close yet so far away in their set up.

In some situations, you may want to consider moving to another home that better suits your care recipient's new needs. With the rising costs of living, this can in fact be a very affordable and functional way to live. Ideally, you will need a home that allows for privacy when desired but also keeps safety at the forefront and aging in place needs in mind, which is no simple task. Consider the suggestions I made earlier in relation to aging in place. I also recommend engaging with a Seniors Real Estate Specialist to help you identify a multi-generational home in your budget.

In addition to the physical arrangement, there is the social one. If your care recipient is your parent, most likely you have not lived with them for many decades, and you both have your own established lives and routines in this stage of life. Your personality, preferences, beliefs, and values have evolved. You may enjoy each other's company, but, coming back to live together now will be very different than it was in the past. Being in each other's space day in and day out can lead to a much higher likelihood for conflicts to arise. No family can say that they are completely void of conflict. Conflicts are normal. However, what is important is how well you can work through disagreements and come to a common ground.

Before plunging into a decision as big as this, it is important to discuss openly your concerns, expectations and desires for how this will work. It might not be an easy conversation to have but addressing these concerns upfront will ensure things go much more smoothly once they are living in your home. Be honest with your care recipient. You will both be giving up something for this new arrangement, and it is a big life adjustment. You will also want to ensure that the financial arrangement is clear and agreed upon. For example, will your care recipient be paying rent? Will they pitch in on bills and other expenses?

You also want to involve the other family members that live in your home as well as those who live elsewhere, such as your spouse, children, and siblings. It is just as important to be open and honest with them. Conducting a family meeting to engage in open discussion may work well for your family. I have included a guide for multi-generational living that will help you formulate your discussion points. If doing this seems daunting, don't be afraid to engage the help of a professional such as an Aging Life Care Manager to help you through the process.

When a grandparent moves in with the adult child and their family, this can understandably throw off the balance in the household and create tensions. However, this arrangement can also encourage bonds between the older and younger members of the family. Some studies have shown that there are great benefits to both the children and grandparents when they are actively engaged in their lives. They will naturally spend more time together, and forge lasting memories. The children tend to develop into more emotionally stable adults who are more socially equipped, and the grandparents could benefit by adding an average of five years to their lives. Research indicates that time spent with grandchildren can reduce risks associated with chronic illnesses and keep older adults physically and mentally healthy. Furthermore, grandparents can make great babysitters for busy parents! Just be sure that child care arrangements are a topic of discussion in advance, so there is no confusion or hard feelings about expectations. Remember that children may need to be explained more about their grandparent's medical or cognitive condition(s) to help them better understand why they are moving in and how it may affect them.

At first, once your care recipient is settled in and you adjust to your new "normal," your new caregiving role may seem quite manageable. Your care recipient's condition may even drastically improve in the new, more supportive setting. However, you may recall in the beginning of this book I spoke about the "slippery slope" of caregiving. When moving a care recipient into your home, even if they are relatively independent at the onset, this becomes an even greater risk. It is important to keep a finger on the pulse of the level of burden, and to know when it is the right time to reach out to the support team you have put in place for a lifeline for help. Family and friends tend to offer more help in the beginning, checking in frequently. They may assist with things like grocery shopping, meal prep and doctor's appointments. In some families this may continue, but for many it tends to dissipate over time.

Either way, as the primary caregiver, as your care recipient becomes increasingly dependent you are the one who is going to bear the greatest burden. For those who work outside of the home, this can mean a real strain on your career. Remember that one of my five tips for caregivers is setting boundaries. As we discussed previously, you need to decide what your threshold is for how much care you are able and willing to provide to your care recipient. Before you reach that limit it is better to put support in place to ensure you don't cross over that line. Read on for more insight regarding in-home support.

IN HOME SUPPORT

Whether your care recipient lives on their own or has moved in with you, there may come a time that they require support above and beyond what you can provide. You may wonder when is the right time to bring in additional help. What should you look for to determine if it is the right time to bring elder-care services into the home? Reference the included checklist for some of the "red flags" that can be indicators that more assistance is needed. If you do notice some of these signs the best action to take is to discuss your concerns with your care recipient and potential next steps.

Fortunately the range of services available to someone who wants to age in place continues to expand. The availability of these services has enabled many more people, even those living with complex medical illnesses, to live at home with a higher quality of life than ever before. There is also a push from a legislative standpoint for broader coverage by Medicare and other insurances, which will make aging in place easier for many people. Do however bear in mind that the options available to your care recipient will vary based on their insurance coverage, geographical area, and other factors.

Let's start by discussing the types of supportive care. You may find that any number of the following services are available:

Adult day care centers. If no one is home during the day to help care for your care recipient, you may want to consider adult day care for safety reasons. Day centers offer supportive care, meals and activities in a facility usually during normal "business hours"(although some offer evening and weekend hours as well). Additionally, some provide transportation to and from home. This can be very beneficial to a caregiver who also works during the day. Technically, this service is not "in-home", but utilizing it can help you keep your care recipient at home.

Some adult day care centers are run by nonprofit organizations, many of which are associated with senior centers and/or churches. Some are specialized for people with dementia, providing them with a safe and supportive environment.

In-home care. First, there is an important distinction between home health care and in-home care. Most often when the term "Home Health care" is being used by a professional such as a physician or a social worker, what they mean is services that are more medical in nature, such as Nursing, Physical, Occupational or Speech Therapy. These services are initiated based on medical need, require a physician order, and are paid for by Medicare and other insurance. This type of home health is intermittent and temporary in nature, however. It is fortunate that through expanding home health care companies, a wide range of services can be provided in the home, such as therapy, wound care, laboratory tests and diagnostics, infusion support, mobile pharmacy services, nutritional support, social services, visiting physician services and more.

However, "in-home care" usually references basic companion care, provided by home care aides. This service is not something that Medicare and other major insurance companies currently cover. As your care recipient's primary caregiver, you may find yourself managing tasks ranging from grocery shopping and meal prep to medications and doctor's appointments. Bringing in a home care aide may be just the support you need to keep them safe and thriving at home. In-home care exists to fill the gaps, and to help people manage their day-to-day needs that cannot be met by family members or other support networks. In -home care companies employ caregivers who go to the client's home and provide these services and the clients pay for the services privately, so that they can continue to live in the comfort of home as they get older. The home care aide can assist with the ADLs and IADLs we talked about in an earlier chapter. As a refresher, ADLs include things like bathing, dressing and ambulation, while IADLs include things such as laundry, light housekeeping and meal preparation. Additionally, the added socialization and engagement that they will experience by having a home care aide can be very beneficial.

Countless clients of my home care agency have had home care aides who became like a part of the family and remain so even after the care recipient's passing. In this way the benefits of in-home care have a long-lasting positive effect. But, it isn't for everyone, and it isn't always a permanent long-term solution. Later in this chapter I will provide additional insight into ways to ensure your in-home care experience is a successful one.

Live-in Home Care. You might be considering 24-hour care for your care recipient. If so, consider an agency that provides live-in caregivers. Live-in care is around-the-clock care, but it is different from 24-hour care. A live-in care provider physically lives on the premises of the client. Live-in care can be a cost-effective alternative to residential or nursing home placement—for clients who live alone, or with a spouse that is unable to care for them on their own. For those who need at least ten or more hours of care each day, it can provide the needed peace of mind for family caregivers to know that someone is always there to help. By being charged on a live-in basis, and not hourly, this can be a substantial money saver for you. It also provides added peace of mind that someone is consistently there around the clock for your care recipient. States have varying laws about how live in care is handled from an employment standpoint so it is important to be aware of those laws before engaging in live in home care.

Hospice Care. Hospice is for people with a terminal diagnosis and limited life expectancy, who are no longer receiving curative treatment. The focus of hospice is on comfort and quality of life rather than recovery. Hospice can be provided anywhere the patient is,whether that is a private home, senior community, nursing home or any other location. I once knew of a patient that a local hospice company supported who was living under a bridge. Even if someone has no insurance or financial means, hospice will be there for them.

Hospice care is more than just nursing care. The team that will work with the patient often includes an array of professionals in addition to a nurse, such as a physician, nurse's aide, social worker, chaplain, volunteers, and bereavement counselors. Hospice provides the medications, equipment and supplies deemed necessary to manage the hospice diagnosis and keep the patient comfortable. The goals are individualized based on the patient's diagnosis, individual living situation and needs. This includes the needs of the support persons and/or family. Additionally, bereavement services are even provided to the family long after the patient has passed.

It is important to remember that while Hospice can provide an array of life-enhancing services, much like skilled home health care, hospice is intermittent and temporary. At times, if symptoms are intensified, Medicare will authorize hospice to provide temporary shifts of 24-hour care in the home until the symptoms are managed. This type of around-the-clock support is not typical of hospice and is not generally provided for more than a few days, until the patient either stabilizes or passes away. Oftentimes people need more help than what is covered by Hospice under Medicaid. Frequently, non-medical home care will need to be brought in alongside Hospice to fill the gaps.

For someone who lives in a senior living community, Hospice can provide much needed support to the care team in the facility. Not only will the Hospice team take some of the burden for caring for the patient off the facility staff, but they will also be an additional set of eyes and ears to keep you up to date on your care recipient's condition. There are so many examples from my career of where I have seen Hospice make a drastic difference for people living in senior living communities, but one in particular stands out. Jim's mother Shirley was a client of my home care agency. While she lived in an assisted living community, she had services from a home care aide in the mornings to provide extra help. Shirley was always an exquisite dresser. She wore her hair neatly and always put on her make-up meticulously. She was no longer able to do those things for herself and the staff in the assisted living lacked the time to help her to the extent she desired. So, Jim engaged us to provide that added support as he knew looking her best every day was important to her. After Shirley would get dressed and ready for the day, she and her caregiver would enjoy breakfast and the morning paper together before the caregiver's shift would end. One day, Jim called me in tears. Shirley was in the hospital and they were recommending Hospice care for her upon her return to assisted living. He was devastated because he loved his mom dearly, and the mention of hospice had him understandably shaken. He didn't understand how his mom had taken a turn for the worse so quickly. Unfortunately, the doctors told him that Shirley had been having a series of mini strokes that were causing the rapid deterioration. He understood this, but he knew his mom had recovered from mini strokes in the past that she had rehabilitated from. He expressed that the idea of having her enrolled in hospice seemed like a death sentence to him in our conversation. I assured Jim that engaging with Hospice was the right thing to do if it was what the doctors were recommending. Shirley was much older than the last time she had the mini strokes, and her condition was even more frail. She was not even walking on her own at this point. I told him that Hospice was going to be a blessing to him because while he visited her daily, he could not be there all the time. The more added support he had in caring for her the better. I also told him that should she show signs of improvement they could always stop Hospice care and proceed with rehabilitation. Reluctantly, he agreed. This phone call occurred on black Friday. She returned to her assisted living the next day with Hospice in place. The weeks that followed were filled with family visits, music therapy, pet therapy, chaplains and many other blessings. She passed right after Christmas. Jim was delighted to have had the opportunity to enjoy one last holiday season with his mom and the support from Hospice made all the difference in her quality of life during that time.

As Jim and Shirley's story demonstrates, accepting hospice does not equate to giving up! Engage with hospice as soon as your care recipient is eligible. Many people think of Hospice as a service only for the final days or hours of someone's life, when they are actively passing. However, the benefit is actually available to provide loving support for up to six months. Did you know sometimes people even graduate from Hospice? If their condition stabilizes or improves (which sometimes it does from having the added support) the hospice patient can actually be discharged from hospice and they still have the benefit to use later when their symptoms return or worsen.

My final piece of advice when it comes to hospice is to not delay. The only regret you will have about engaging hospice is that you didn't do it sooner. Hospice is a benefit that your care recipient is entitled to and it can make all the difference in their final days, weeks, months or years. The relief you will feel having this support team in place will be intangible. I have never worked with a patient or their family who regretted their decision to bring in hospice.

ENGAGING WITH IN-HOME CARE

As mentioned already, engaging with dependable in-home care providers can truly make all the difference, especially if your goal is to keep your care recipient at home long- term. It is important to remember that not all agencies are created equal and it is not a one-size-fits-all type of service. When interviewing a home care agency, ask a lot of questions so you can learn about what they offer and how they operate. Knowing the answers helps you to choose an agency that is the best fit, and to know what to expect while working with them. See the checklist I put together on Interviewing In-Home Care Agencies for more guidance.

There are a lot of benefits to using a reputable home care agency. But with so many in-home care agencies out there, how can you tell if the agency you are considering is legitimate? You will want to ensure that the agency you choose meets the standards for which you are paying them to meet. Such standards include:

· Screening: You are relying on the home care company to validate that the home care aide they hire is who they say they are, that their credentials are valid and licenses are up to date.

· Accountability: As an employee of the home care company, the caregiver is held to the professional standards of the industry, company, and licensing agencies. They are accountable to a management hierarchy that will ensure that they are meeting these standards, and addressing any areas where they need improvement.

· Background Transparency: The agency will run pre-employment background checks and often continue post- employment to conduct routine background checks on the caregivers that they employ.

- Reliability: Agencies are constantly hiring. This means they have a bench of caregivers ready and able to work when they need them. Should your caregiver be unable to report to work for a shift, they will work to find a suitable replacement for the shift. They often cannot guarantee it, but you at least have the peace of mind they are working on your behalf.

- Training: Agencies are required to provide ongoing supervision and training of the caregivers they employ. This means continuing education to keep their credential current, hone their skills and address areas needed for professional development.

How do you find one? If you have an advocacy team in place, be sure to reach out to those professionals for referrals. You can also ask for referrals from friends, neighbors, anyone who you know that has used this type of service in the past. If you don't know where to start, you are likely to be able to secure a list of some of the local area's reputable companies from the Area Agency on Aging or from the social work department at a local hospital. The National Association for Home Care and Hospice also has an online agency locator,[28] on which agencies pay a fee to be listed, but they do undergo a certain level of vetting first. Once you have connected with an agency, check out their website—does it look professional and provide up-to-date information? Do they have good reviews from past clients? The agency should also be able to provide you with referrals from their community partners and past clients.

Pricing will vary, so it is prudent to call around and get a feel for the average pricing in your area. You will not want to choose based on price alone, but you do want to be an educated consumer and know that you are not overpaying for what you receive. You will also want to know if pricing is all-inclusive, or if there are any add-on charges. Like anything else, you can expect to get what you pay for. To have confidence that you will receive quality services, what you are looking for is an in-home care agency that will truly partner with you in the care of your care recipient. This means not just getting your care recipient's address and sending the first available person with a pulse to their home. It means that they will listen to what your care recipient's needs are, match them with an

[28] agencylocator.nahc.org

appropriate and compassionate caregiver to meet their needs, and work with you to manage any situation that comes up that may jeopardize the aging in place plan. Most in-home care agencies will offer a free consultation to help you assess the situation and provide guidance in your decision-making process. They should conduct an assessment of your needs as well as wants and preferences, and this information should be relayed to your assigned caregiver(s). The agency should help to orient that caregiver to your household needs and expectations, and hold them accountable to it as well.

One of the primary benefits of using a reputable agency is having the management's involvement in ensuring that the caregiver does what they are supposed to do and, if not, they work to replace them with another suitable option. A good agency will stay in touch with you and perform occasional in-person visits to get feedback as to how your caregiver is working out and address any issues or concerns that come up in a timely manner. You should always feel comfortable reaching out to the management if your caregiver is not meeting your expectations.

Finding a good fit in a home care aide is important, but it can be very hard to determine who will be a good fit from day one. When I had my home care agency, for the first few years I would arrange in-person interviews for every care recipient and their family with the home care aides I had available that I felt were a good match for them. Over time, I stopped doing that because in most cases, the first impression was not an accurate representation of the aide/care recipient match. The home care aide was nervous, usually responding to the questions that the family peppered them with, sometimes struggling with language barriers or cultural differences. For this reason, I recommend trusting your home care agency to match for your care recipient. They get to know the home care aides on a deeper level, and they build and understanding of the types of clients each are best suited for as they work with them.

The only situation that I recommend insisting on in-person interviews is when you are engaging a live-in caregiver. With a live-in arrangement, it is even more important to find a good match upfront. This person is going to be moving into your care recipient's home. They will be spending a significant amount of time with your care recipient. One reason I recommend the in person interview is so that the home care aide can see the living environment. Bear in mind that you must provide a separate bedroom and bathroom to bathe in. They also must be given down time and be able to get enough uninterrupted rest. Many people utilize an alert monitoring system so that if the client does end up needing assistance at night while the care provider is resting, they are still able to alert them. This works much like a baby monitor with two-way communication. This can work well, but if the caregiver is interrupted consistently every night, they may not be able to get adequate sleep. Additionally, there are other important conversations to have up front. Some examples may include: what spaces in the home are considered private, how to handle personal phone calls, where to store personal belongings, and how and when the caregiver will eat, bathe and tend to personal errands. It is crucial to take your time and not make a rushed decision. Doing so, along with detailed preparation and open communication will make the experience that much more comfortable for everyone involved. These actions will help ensure an easier transition for everyone. Most live-in caregivers do end up becoming like extended family and the experience can be very rewarding for both parties.

Once you have what seems like a good fit, setting expectations up front is one of the most important tools for successful implementation of in-home care. It will ensure the caregiver knows what is required of them and avoids uncomfortable misunderstandings later. A reputable agency will create what is called a care plan upon admission. This care pan usually involves getting an inventory of the medical and care needs of your care recipient. It is less likely to include non-medical support or even less common, social aspects. Be sure to be proactive about providing information about your care recipient socially, emotionally, and spiritually, even if they don't ask! Furthermore, ask for a copy of the care plan. Then, when your caregiver begins working, be sure to ask if they have seen the care plan. If they have not (which is very common), give them a copy and go over it with them to see if they have any questions or concerns you can discuss with them to help them know and understand your care recipient better.

Remember, you are in control and the in-home care agency is obligated to work with you to find a suitable replacement if the first one does not work out. Sometimes, it takes two or three tries to find the right match! Give each potential match at least a week's worth of shifts before you decide about compatibility. If it seems at first to be difficult, I will implore you to be patient and let them go through their processes. It is much easier to stick with an agency through the "working out the kinks" process in the beginning and give them the chance to get it right versus jumping from one to the next and having to start all over again.

When it comes to the scheduling part, there is often a discrepancy up front between the number of hours the care recipient or their caregiver feels they need and the number of hours the care agency feels they need. Often when talking with clients during my time in the home care industry I would receive the question, "I know we need help, but I am not sure what the caregiver will DO all day when they are not providing my [care recipient] physical assistance?" Many older adults need assistance with personal care, and those needs are intermittent and spread throughout the day. For example, most of the time a care recipient's morning routine involves some level of physical assistance— taking a shower, getting dressed, and grooming – but after those tasks are completed, what does the caregiver do until the next physical need arises (perhaps going to the bathroom)? Well, first and foremost, both ADLs and IADLs are necessary for an elder individual to function on a day-to-day basis and remain as independent as possible in their own home. When there is no ADL needing to be attended to, the caregiver can assist with IADLs. This may include tasks like meal preparation, light housekeeping and laundry, linen changes, sorting/opening mail, and even transportation to appointments, shopping, and other activities. Some older adults may be fully dependent on others to perform these tasks while others may need minimal supervision or assistance. Either way, a home care aide can help ensure these essential tasks are done.

Generally, in-home care is more expensive the less you use. It is like buying in bulk; the more hours you buy, the less the cost is per hour. But potential consumers can be hesitant to purchase more hours of in-home care because they are unsure of how to fill those hours and they don't want the caregiver to be just "sitting around." They are missing one of the most important things with this perspective! When there is a good caregiver and care recipient match, once ADL and IADL needs have been met, the "down time" can be filled with what is perhaps the most important service that a caregiver can offer—joyful companionship. Just having someone to talk to, have a cup of tea and read the paper with, or enjoy a board game can provide much needed socialization for lonely individuals and goes a long way in staving off symptoms of depression. Remember Maslow's hierarchy? Furthermore, the caregiver is also serving as "eyes and ears" for family who may not be able to be there which provides a peace of mind that in my personal opinion you cannot put a price tag on.

REGISTRIES

Due to the rising costs of in-home care, many older adults and their families consider hiring a caregiver through a registry or an online directory to save money. Unfortunately, people don't usually understand the difference between a registry and an in-home care agency. I am not saying that using a registry should never be done. However, you should know that hiring from a registry means that you will not enjoy the benefits I outlined above that using a reputable home care agency will provide. As an advocate for aging and disabled adults, I am primarily concerned with consumers being educated on what they are buying. The lower price, while attractive, means you are paying for something that is less than and therefore, you may experience problems.

First, anyone can say they are a "nurse" or "nurse aide". A lot of people don't know the difference between an aide, nursing assistant, and nurse. In many states there are only certain credentials that will qualify someone to be considered suitable for employment by a licensed home care agency. When you are hiring privately, you are unlikely to know the difference or to be able to verify the credentials. If you hire a caregiver without the proper skills or training, this becomes a very risky situation.

In a private hire arrangement, a caregiver is solely responsible for keeping licenses active and credentials up to date and quite often these things fall to the wayside. There is also no training or supervision provided by a professional. Furthermore, background checks can be confusing, expensive and time-consuming. If you do not perform one at all you are taking a big risk of allowing a stranger into your home. And just like credentialing, there are many different types and levels of background checks that licensed agencies routinely do, which include information a basic local background check would not uncover.

Finally, in a private hire situation, you are becoming an employer. Many people do not fully understand the implications of this arrangement. As an employer one is responsible for taxes, unemployment insurance, and liability for both the caregiver's and care recipient's physical safety while care is being provided. It is also important to know that there are federal rules and also rules in many states that govern how home care is treated from an employment standpoint. You must ensure that you are following those rules and you are protected from any employer related liabilities. Do keep in mind that there are even more stringent legal requirements that govern live-in care. They must be given appropriate accommodations and schedules. This must be monitored and revisited on a regular basis. There is also little to no recourse if the home care aide you hire privately does not show up for a shift, and there is rarely a back-up plan when this occurs. There is no management other than yourself to help resolve issues when they come up and to routinely evaluate your caregiver's performance.

If you do decide to hire privately, it is important to make sure you protect yourself. Remember that it is both the care recipient and you, the caregiver (especially if you have legal standing as Power of Attorney or Agent) that is on the hook if something goes wrong. You can be held personally accountable as an employer. Make sure that you cover yourself from a tax, insurance and legal standpoint. It is prudent to use a reputable payroll service to pay your caregiver. Also, be sure to communicate thoroughly and *document everything* well. This means schedules, pay rates, time-off requests, reported issues at work, any workplace complaints or concerns, performance issues, and a multitude of other things.

No matter how you locate and hire your in-home caregiver, you may have concerns about safety, especially if you are not going to be present when they are with your care recipient. A good approach is to let the caregiver know you will be checking in on a monitor camera. Sometimes these are referred to as nanny cams. This can give you the peace of mind that you can check in on your care recipient throughout the day, without necessarily interrupting care services in the way a telephone call may be disruptive.

Despite the most valiant efforts by the home care agency, caregivers and support system, sometimes in-home care fails. In this section I will outline some of the most common reasons I have observed. By being aware of them and preparing in advance, you will be better equipped to avoid these common pitfalls.

One of the primary reasons home care doesn't work out is the inability to locate a suitable and consistent caregiver. While home care agencies generally do put their best effort into hiring and maintaining consistency with the staff they match with care recipients, the nature of the business is extremely inconsistent. The inconsistency of staffing is one of the top complaints by consumers of in-home care services. The unreliability, even if it is rare, is burdensome when the care recipient cannot be alone without a caregiver. Moreover, the pain felt by staff turnover in the home setting is exponentially greater than that felt when staff turnover happens in senior living. I am sure you can imagine that once your care recipient is accustomed to someone who is day in and day out attending to their most intimate needs, the disruption of losing that person is devastating. In senior living, the care recipients get accustomed to a team of caregivers so losing one that they are comfortable with might still be painful, but it is a smoother transition to have another familiar face there ready to assist.

Another reason in-home care might fail is that the home is not conducive to increasing care needs. As we discussed earlier in this chapter, many homes, particularly older ones, are simply not suitable for aging in place. If the environment has not been properly outfitted and equipped for the disabilities your care recipient may experience as they become more dependent on professional caregivers, it will be frustrating to both parties. The caregivers will inevitably become fearful that their care recipient is unsafe in their environment and it is not fair to expect professional caregivers to work in an environment that is unsafe. Sometimes the determination is made that the investment that would be necessary to upgrade the home is not feasible.

In addition to the environment being unsafe, complex medical needs are another reason in-home care may be unsuccessful. As we reviewed in chapter two, your care recipient may have greater medical needs over time. And while professional home care may be able to alleviate the burden for a while, there is a limit to what they can handle as well. This leads into the final point I will make about home care failures which is the potential for it to become cost prohibitive. Oftentimes as care needs reach a peak, the cost of in-home care becomes cost-prohibitive. Around the clock home care gets expensive, quickly. This may be because of a combination of factors: increasing hours, the higher salary of a professional caregiver with the level of skill necessary to provide the care they require, and also because of the costs of supplies and equipment necessary to meet their needs.

Finally, sometimes home care fails because the care recipient (or their spouse) is resistant to making it work. Here are some tactics to try when introducing a hired caregiver to a resistant care recipient:

- Introduce the caregiver as a "housekeeper" or "driver".
- Set it up as a social interaction.
- Tell your care recipient you can't make it so you asked so and so to drop in and check on them, bring them food, etc

Of course, there are other factors that could lead to the failure of an in-home care plan. It is critical to rely on the expertise of your advocacy team to address hurdles as they arise. However, there may come a time when you determine that it is safest, most cost effective, or easiest for everyone involved for your care recipient to live and receive care in a senior living setting.

OPTIONS FOR SENIOR LIVING

As I mentioned in an earlier chapter, one of the most common concerns I have heard from family caregivers is, "I promised mom or dad I would never put him or her in a nursing home." If this is you, I understand and respect your desire to keep that promise. However, sometimes senior living is truly the safest option for an aging, frail or disabled adult. The biggest piece of advice I have for you is to not let the fear of breaking a promise paralyze you. Frequently the only regret is not doing it sooner!

Bear in mind the perception of "nursing home" that your care recipient had in mind when they made this request is probably outdated. The reality is there are a number of choices of senior living lifestyles that are nothing like the "nursing homes" of the past. They also most likely were not able to think ahead into the future and imagine the burden this promise would put on you and your family. Therefore, my first piece of advice is to not let the guilt cloud your decision. Instead, put your energy into finding a place where your care recipient will be safe, cared for, loved, and enjoy a high quality of life.

Sometimes placement in a senior living community can be a temporary solution in a situation such as debilitating illness or injury, to allow time for additional planning to be made for a safe return home. When faced with making a decision quickly in a situation such as this, your choices may be limited, and you may not have the luxury of time to do in depth research.

Choosing a senior living community for your care recipient to call home on a permanent basis will take some more serious consideration. In most scenarios, older adults only move into senior living as a last resort. There are many things you can do as their support person to make it easier, starting with the decision-making process.

First, let's start with one of my five tips for caregivers – educate yourself. It is important to explore the different types of senior living communities available for your care recipient. If you don't know there is a difference between a nursing home and an assisted living facility, you are not alone. The differences vary as much in types of senior living communities as fingerprints do in humans. So, how do you know which is best for your care recipient or where to start? First it is important to understand the medical model versus the social model.

Nursing homes are based on a medical model. In many ways they are like mini hospitals in both design and operation. Most people think of a nursing home when they think of long term care. They are not the most inviting environments for someone to want to call home for the last several years of their life. Nevertheless, the level of skilled nursing these facilities provide often cannot be provided at home so, in some cases residents must reside in this setting in order to have their needs met. When medical needs require a skilled eye around the clock, placement in a skilled nursing facility will most likely be the best option. This is because it will become exhausting both for family caregivers and financially difficult to pay for in-home care. Often there is a tipping point where nursing home care makes better financial and practical sense. Nursing homes are subsidized by federal funds so that older adults who need this level of care are able to receive it long term.

As we discussed in an earlier chapter, many nursing homes today house a high percentage of short-term residents who are recovering post-hospitalization, with the intention of returning to their home environment. The money received from Medicare for these short term stays is generally much higher than the private pay or Medicaid long term care rates, making this business model desirable to most nursing home operators.

Assisted living is something completely different. Gerontologist Dr. Keren Brown is generally recognized as the founder of the assisted living model. She was in graduate school in the mid 1970s when her mother had a stroke, putting her in a nursing home, which she hated. Her mother's medical needs were being met, however, she observed that she was being treated like a "patient" and not like a person. For instance, there was very little to engage or encourage her in between medication passes and therapy treatments. By her estimation, there were likely to be a lot of older adults like her mother who needed custodial support, but not skilled care. Therefore, she set out to create a model that would offer a level of care that was supportive but more home-like and provided for the social and emotional needs of the resident in addition to the medical. It is a person-centered model. In 1981 she opened Park Place Assisted Living in Portland, Oregon, which is recognized as the first modern assisted living community in the United States.[29] If you would like to know more about Karen's story, check out the book Being Mortal by Atul Gawande (listed in the index).

Since Dr. Brown pioneered the model, assisted living has continued to evolve

---

[29] encyclopedia.com/books/politics-and-business-magazines/assisted-living-concepts-inc

to meet the needs of seniors in the U.S. Today there are numerous types of senior living communities that exist, offering an array of services and amenities. Let's start by narrowing down the categories into those that are the most common in today's landscape of options.

Active Living/Independent Living Communities. These communities are usually age-restricted, (generally 55+) and minors are prohibited from being permanent residents. Residences usually include single-family homes or condominiums that are either owned by the tenant or rented on a monthly basis, and amenities such as an exercise facility, clubhouse, golf courses, tennis courts, walking trails, business centers, and pools are often available. HOA fees usually include a higher level of general maintenance and security than your average neighborhood. These communities are not health care facilities. The residents should live independent lifestyles but if care is needed, they would need to locate, hire and utilize said care in their own private residence. Some independent living communities do however offer some contracted services on site.

Assisted Living. Assisted Living Communities are licensed by the state to provide levels of assistance with daily activities such as bathing, dressing, toileting, transferring, and medication administration. While they are not 24-hour nursing facilities, most do offer some level of nursing supervision and presence daily. This type of community typically offers varying options for apartment layouts, but bear in mind you are trading off personal space with the security of having staff available around the clock to help if needed. Usually included in rent are some or all meals, served in a common dining space; housekeeping services; laundry; exercise programs; and recreational activities. Some are all-inclusive while others work on more of an a-la-carte model. There may be additional charges for an increased level of care services on an as-needed basis. This type of community is mostly only able to be paid for by private pay or long-term care insurance although in some states there are federally funded Medicaid waiver programs available.

Memory Care. Memory care is a type of assisted living community, offering disease-specific care from staff who have been trained to work with patients suffering from memory impairments such as Alzheimer's. These are generally secure facilities, meaning that the residents are not free to come and go as they please. This is for safety reasons.

Board and Care Homes/Residential Care Homes- The availability and licensing of Board and Care homes vary greatly across the United States. In most states, they are required to be licensed in some fashion. The facilities themselves are typically residential houses that have been modified, making them more home-like than a lot of their assisted living facility competitors. They are also generally limited in the number of residents they can house and provide care for. However, like assisted living, they are staffed around the clock and in addition to room and board, provide support services such as ADL care and medication management. For some, the home-like environment and lower staff to resident ratio make this type of senior living a preferred choice. However, these facilities can be limited in their ability to provide medical services on-site, engaging activities, transportation and other benefits that larger assisted living communities are more suited to offer. Like Assisted Living, this type of community is mostly only able to be paid for by private pay or long-term care insurance depending on the type of licensing they have.

Nursing Homes/Skilled Nursing Facilities. As we already discussed earlier when we talked about hospitalizations, a nursing home (otherwise known as a skilled nursing facility, or SNF) is licensed to provide around the clock nursing care for those who need a higher level of care. Because it is a medical model, and the residents are some of the most frail and sick elderly, the facility must have a licensed physician always on call. These communities meet all the same custodial needs as Assisted Living, and have the capability to provide more intensive medical care as needed. As discussed in an earlier chapter, some individuals go into Skilled Nursing Facilities short term, to receive intensive therapy following an illness or injury so they can gain strength to return home. Others, who need this level of care constantly, may become permanent residents of the nursing home. Nursing homes generally do accept state and federal funding. Lack of privacy, the hospital-like environment, and low-quality dining options are the most common complaints. However, like Assisted Living, Nursing homes have also come a long way in the past several decades, expanding upon the social and emotional support offered to the residents. Many modern facilities now offer private rooms and bathrooms, the residents enjoy more robust activities programs, and therapy services provided on site are often excellent.

Continuing Care Retirement Communities (CCRC's). This type of community often combines any or all of the aforementioned levels of care. The services are generally not all offered under one roof, therefore the residents receiving care would have to move from one area of the community to another as their care needs change. There are many different types of contracts for CCRCs but most consist of a Buy-In Structure and/or Monthly Payment Structure.

It is important to note that the distinction between the medical model and the social model has blurred significantly over the past several years. As life expectancies increase and the baby boomers come of age, the demand for long-term care services has skyrocketed. This has caused a domino effect in the senior living industry to provide a higher level of care in each setting. Hospitals are overloaded, discharging more people to skilled nursing facilities, therefore skilled nursing facilities must provide a significantly higher level of care to keep patients from going back to the hospital. Assisted living facilities, as their residents desire to age in place, have been forced to incorporate a higher level of medical care into their model, often contracting services such as visiting physicians to see residents who can no longer go out and home health, therapy and hospice providers to provide on-site services to their residents. And in turn more and more support services are being modified to be offered in the home setting as well.

TOURING SENIOR LIVING FACILITIES

In seeking out senior living options, it is not a good idea to take your care recipient everywhere you consider. This would likely overwhelm them. First, narrow down your search by location, price, and business model. This can be hard to do without help. Soliciting the assistance of a geriatric care manager or assisted living placement specialist could be extremely helpful. If you are already using in-home care, ask the nurse or administrator for guidance. Chances are, they have clients who have transitioned to them and perhaps even provide services in some, so they are likely to have helpful information they can share. And again, checking with your advocacy team and getting their recommendations is always an excellent strategy. Next, do some of the research and touring on your own first, and pare down to a short list of communities that you think they will like.

How do you narrow it down? My best advice is to start with state surveys. These are a public record and can tell you a lot about the community and its management. If there are concerns you have from the surveys, these are things to bring up with the management when you tour the facility to learn more about what the issues were and how they resolved them.

Second, drop in for your tour. Do not schedule it ahead of time. The salespeople for the communities you visit won't be happy that I told you to do this, because this way, they have not done all the "staging" for your visit. During an unscheduled visit you will get a better feel for the way the community generally operates. As you wait, take a peek into the common areas. Take note of how the residents look, how the staff interact with them, what is going on in the hallways and common areas, and how clean it is. Be careful not to be fooled by the chandeliers and fancy artwork. The most aesthetically pleasing are not always the most well-run communities.

Finally, be sure to interview the "big 3". This consists of the Executive Director (sometimes called the Administrator), the Director of Nursing (sometimes called Health Care Coordinator or something similar) and the Director of Dining Services (sometimes called Culinary Experience Director or something similar). This may not be possible on your first tour, especially if you drop in. You are going to initially be met by the Salesperson (again, title may vary) and you may be told they are unavailable without an appointment. However, the salesperson is incentivized by the number of people that move in each month, so they are likely to tell you whatever you want to hear to get you to open your checkbook. Unfortunately, this means they often make promises that they cannot keep. So be sure that before you make a decision to place your care recipient in any community that you have the opportunity to speak with all three of these key personnel. Take note of any differences in what they tell you, any areas in which it does not seem they are on the same page. I have included a list of questions to ask each of them in a checklist for this chapter.

Once you have a list of three or four communities that you think your care recipient would like, review the list with them. Go over the options and why you chose them. Ask if your care recipient has any specific "non-negotiables" and if any of those are not met by the ones you chose, cross them off the list. Now is when you want to pre-schedule a time to come back and bring your care recipient. You don't want to drop in when you bring your care recipient because you want the facility to be prepared for them, as your wait time will be less, and they will be prepared for your care recipient's specific needs and concerns based on their previous discussions with you.

As with in-home care, setting realistic expectations up front is the key to successful senior living transitions. You will be well served to start with open, honest communication with the management of the communities you are considering. Work to identify any hot buttons that your care recipient will be concerned about in the beginning and talk through how those concerns will be handled if and when they arise.

During the tour, observe how the management and staff interact with your care recipient and other residents. Encourage your care recipient to ask questions and engage with the staff. Take note of planned activities happening in the community. Do the scheduled activities appear to be happening? DO they seem appropriate for the residents participating? Does the community seem "lively" or is it dull?

You may also find it helpful to ask for a meal while you are visiting. Senior living communities are usually very accommodating with food and drink during a tour. It is a great way to get a taste of what their dining services have to offer. Knowing whether your care recipient will like the style of food service that the community offers is a valuable part of your evaluation. The dining room is also a great place to meet and chat with current residents and their families.

During the tours, take notes and make a list of pros and cons for each community you visit with your care recipient. Afterwards, sit down and discuss the options and determine which one can best meet your care recipient's needs and checks off most of the "pros" column. If your care recipient started with any specific "non-negotiables", do not compromise on them even if the community is a better price or otherwise attractive. Non-negotiables are non-negotiables for a reason. Your care recipient ultimately will not be happy if they concede on any of them.

THE DOWNSIDES OF SENIOR LIVING

Remember that there will be no "perfect fit". Once your care recipient identifies a community that matches most of their preferences, understand that no matter how good the match seems to be there will still be difficulties in transition. I will touch on how to make the transition easier later, but first let's discuss some of the most common challenges related to senior living as a whole. Most of the time it is unrealistic expectations in these key areas that lead to disappointments.

Paying careful attention to these key areas, and not just the decor and amenities, will serve you well in understanding the dynamics of the community and what their capabilities and limitations are. My grandmother used to say you can put lipstick on a pig but it is still a pig. I am sorry for the crude analogy but, the same is true in senior living!

DINING

Food is one of the biggest complaints that older adults have in senior living communities. Although the dining experience in senior living communities has come a long way, the truth is, it is an easy thing to complain about and it is very difficult to reconcile when there are complaints.

Most senior living communities put a strong focus on delivering as close to a fine dining experience as possible. The executives of the larger, more hospitality-focused communities will spare no expense in recruiting dining service talent and food supply budgets.

Find out what the dining options are, and how flexible the menus can be if the resident does not like what is being offered on a given day. It is also important to learn about how they handle any special dietary restrictions your care recipient may have. Medical dietary needs are a priority and should be followed by the dietary team with oversight by a licensed nutritionist. In terms of personal preferences, do keep in mind they are preparing food in bulk. While they will do their best with accommodations, they will not be able to personalize everything for your care recipient upon request. As a caregiver, regularly visiting and having meals with your care recipient will be important for monitoring the quality of the food and service and compliance with any special dietary needs your care recipient has.

Also, note that in senior living communities, it is the mid-day meal that is usually the most substantial. This is because eating a larger meal earlier in the day can help older adults stay energized longer, and because physical activity usually decreases later in the evening, eating a large meal late can cause weight management issues. Furthermore, retiring to bed shortly after a large meal can cause sleep disturbances as the body is struggling to digest the meal during sleep. If having a larger meal at midday and a smaller one in the evening is not preferable for your care recipient, be sure to voice this up front and ask whether accommodations can be made.

Finally remember, three meals a day may or may not be included in the standard pricing, so be sure to find out what is and is not included up front.

STAFFING RATIOS

Most new residents of senior living communities are aware at the start that they will not have their own personal nurse or aide. There are assigned staff for each shift that share the responsibilities of taking care of the varying needs of the residents of the community. The regulatory requirements for staffing ratios vary based on type of facility, licensing and state, but more often than not, care recipients and their families are unpleasantly surprised that they are as high as they are. One nurse aide may be responsible for tens or even dozens of residents. The ratios are particularly high on overnight shifts. The problems that the high ratios cause are slow response times, hurried care and overworked staff.

Care recipients and their families are often even more surprised that their assigned staff have very little credentials and training. In many states there does not have to be a licensed nurse in the building all day every day for assisted living. In some cases there are care aides working with residents who have had 40 hours or less of formal training. Staffing shortages can cause hurried hires, rushed training and minimal supervision.

This particular senior living concern has grown even more worrisome in light of the COVID 19 crisis. However, it is not just senior living that is affected. Staffing shortages are a problem at every level of care, from home care to hospitals to nursing homes and everywhere in between. This is not likely to improve any time soon. Keeping this in mind, recognizing hard working nurses and aides, and showing appreciation for a job well done under a stressful work environment will go a long way. Nurses and aides in senior living facilities tend to regard praise from their residents and families at even higher value than that from their supervisors and bosses. No one goes into this profession without a heart for caring and knowing that the people they are caring for appreciate them makes a world of difference. So while it can be easy to notice and complain when the service is sub-par, try and be equally or more so tuned in to the standout service.

MEDICATION MANAGEMENT

Senior living communities are not usually allowed by regulatory standards for residents to administer their own medications. Even where it is allowed, in most cases the management is going to be reluctant to allow it because of the risks involved. Many new senior living residents are bothered by this because they are accustomed to taking their medications at the same time every day. Because of the volume of medications that need to be given out, the nurses in a senior living community cannot always accommodate the preferred medication times of all residents. They do their best but making accommodations can slow the process down even more; for example if they are running from one side of the building to another to accommodate a particular resident's preferred time, this slows down the entire process.

For the same reasons cited above regarding staffing shortages, medication management delivery suffers as well. Understanding that unless your care recipient has strict medication times for health reasons (such as some Parkinson's medications requiring very strict timing), you will be well served to remain patient and flexible with medication administration as possible. If your care recipient does have a strict medication regimen, this should be discussed at admission and included in their plan of care.

Finally, remember that medication errors are common in the long term care setting, particularly when the care recipient moves from one level of care to the next. So, I remind you to take this seriously and insist upon thorough medication reconciliation every time. Be sure to go over the medication list with your care recipient's care team each time there is a change in status and insist on being informed of any changes in between. Staying on top of this will allow you to be a strong advocate in this area and help catch potential errors before they occur.

BATHING

In most senior living communities, the assisted bathing schedule is on average twice per week per resident. This may not seem like enough for your care recipient, especially if they are accustomed to bathing daily or every other day. It is important to consider that bathing every day is not usually necessary, especially if physical activity level is lower as is the case with most older adults. Too frequent bathing can even sometimes cause health issues such as dry and cracked skin because excessive washing removes oils from the skin. However, in between showers, thorough assistance with personal hygiene and cleansing daily should be provided for all residents.

As a senior living administrator, I found one of the most common complaints from families was that their care recipient was not being bathed frequently enough. When investigating these complaints, I would often find that the staff were documenting bathing refusal by the resident. This is particularly common in memory care, or in assisted living with residents who have cognitive impairments. The care recipient becomes fearful of bathing and when approached by the staff to bathe they say no, sometimes rather aggressively, and instead of working to find a way to encourage the bath with the care recipient, they simply move on to the next. They may become too frustrated or they may simply not want to take the extra time in their packed schedules.

Bathing is an important topic of discussion to determine how the community can or cannot accommodate your care recipient's needs and preferences when it comes to bathing appropriately. If you find your care recipient does begin to refuse bathing, work with the community management as a team to overcome this challenge. You may be able to provide valuable insight into the best way to approach your care recipient about bathing. For example, you can explain your care recipient's normal routine at home to the staff. Did they normally bathe in the morning or at night? Did they take a tub bath or a shower? By aligning the approach to bathing closely to the care recipient's lifelong habits, they are more likely to garner success.

ACTIVITIES

The activities program is a vital part of the lifestyle that a senior living community offers. Be sure you ask for a copy of the activity calendar and review it with your care recipient. Are there activities every day, including weekends, or just during the week? Does the activity calendar reflect events that your care recipient would enjoy? Much like with dining, your care recipient is going to have their own preferences that they are going to want met with the activities program. While it is possible they might pick up and enjoy a new hobby, just like they might try and decide they like a new cuisine, they are still going to want the comfort of activities they always enjoyed. Therefore, you want to determine if the community you are considering offers the types of activities your care recipient enjoys.

You should expect to see a range of activities that will meet the varying needs of a diverse senior living population. The calendar should include activities that encompass a wide range of categories such as physical/recreational exercise, mental stimulation, artistic and musical expression, outdoor/nature enjoyment, spiritual and faith related, and of course encouragement of socialization.

Furthermore, the Director of Activities should take feedback from the residents and cater the activities to the unique wants and preferences of the population they are serving, instead of creating a calendar and expecting everyone to take part in things they may or may not have interest in. In many states, a resident council is a regulatory requirement. Usually, the Director of Activities will facilitate the resident council meetings. You may want to ask to see resident council minutes or at least find out whether the community has one and talk to some of the residents that are a part of it. It is important for the residents to feel that they have input and control over the decisions made in the community.

While I did not include this role in the "big 3", you may also want to ask the Director of Activities (sometimes called the Resident Engagement Director or something similar) a few questions. For example, what do they do when a resident is isolating themselves and rarely or never participates in activities? How do they adjust over time to meet the needs of residents as they become less mobile or experience cognitive impairments? Understanding how the facility approaches these types of challenges will serve you well if and when you face challenges with your care recipient in this area.

WHEN A COUPLE NEEDS CARE

Understandably, it is often a primary concern for couples who have been married for a long time to stay together. It is not uncommon for the healthier spouse to be caring for the other whose medical condition has declined. Many times, the health (both physical and mental) of the caregiving spouse begins to falter and at some point, the family discovers that both spouses are in need of care. A compounding challenge is that their care needs may differ, a scenario that in my experience as an assisted living administrator was one of the biggest challenges to overcome. The family would demand to know if they would be able to stay together. The short-term answer was usually yes, we could place them in a double room together and they would each be assigned their individual appropriate level of care. However, if their needs were to change at different paces, sometimes long-term staying together was not a viable option. This is particularly true when related to a dementia diagnosis. Knowing this made several of the potential residents I spoke with fearful of the unknown future and they would decide they couldn't move forward knowing that possibility existed. Another frequent concern they and their families had was the potential for a greater decline in the healthier parent at the expense of the sicker parent getting the care level that they need. Lastly, the cost of securing two "beds" (even if they really only need one) in a senior living community can also be too taxing on the budget.

One couple in particular comes to mind who moved into the assisted living where I worked, Bill and Delores. When they moved in, their two daughters informed us that their mother, who had moderate Alzheimer's and was wheelchair-bound, was very social and loved being around friends. They were certain she would make friends easily. Their father, on the other hand, was a loner, and preferred that he and his wife remain in their room and not be bothered. However, the daughters thought that he should also be socializing and making friends. And, as they always wanted to be together, they asked that we always ensure that they made it to the group activities. It was a constant struggle, attempting to provide Delores enough active engagement and keeping Bill happy. Eventually, we got them into a good routine but it seemed the daughters were never satisfied. It was difficult to communicate to them that they need not try and change their parents, and to let us work with them each in the way they were comfortable.

Senior living communities with strong, committed leadership that are willing to take creative approaches can make this work. But, due to these challenges, oftentimes home care can be a better solution for couples. In a situation where the healthier spouse is the caregiver, it gives them a much-needed break while they can stick with their normal routine in their usual environment. If both spouses need care, home care agencies are often more flexible to tailor a solution that works best for the individuals, vs. the clients having to adjust to a more rigid care model set up in a senior living community. Many agencies will offer adjusted "couple" rates if one client needs basic companion care such as medication reminders and meal preparation, while the other has more intense personal care needs. This solution can stretch funds much longer for the clients and enable them to both receive the care they need without separating.

SENIOR LIVING TRANSITION

DOWNSIZING AND MOVING COORDINATION

When a decision has been made to move your care recipient, whether it be downsizing, moving in with you, or transitioning to assisted living, the challenges are bigger than just the actual packing and physical logistics of the move.

There is usually a significant amount of purging and decluttering that needs to be done if they are downsizing significantly. Your care recipient has likely lived in their home for quite some time, so they are going to have a lot of "stuff" accumulated. Keep in mind that to your care recipient, it isn't just "stuff". There are memories and sentiments attached to their belongings. They are not going to be able to keep everything that has sentimental value, so there are going to be some tough, emotional decisions to be made over what to keep and what to get rid of.

This is a good opportunity for many older adults to give family heirlooms and sentimental items to loved ones now, while they are alive to enjoy seeing these items passed down. However, some may worry about who should get what or have concerns about fighting. For others, it may be hurtful to learn that loved ones do not have interest in inheriting the item that they intend to pass down. I have four sets of china in my basement. One from my mother, one from my grandmother, one from my husband's mother and one from my husband's aunt. I do not want or use any of them! Nevertheless, I cannot part with them. Each set meant something to the family member that passed them to me, and I honor their sentiment. One day I hope to pass them to my daughters in law who will also have no use for them. My point is that from generation to generation there won't necessarily be the same value placed on items and this can cause discord, so it is important to remember that tensions can run high in these situations and feelings can be hurt.

Another issue that is common to face in this process is hoarding. Hoarding is technically a medical diagnosis that is quite rare, but it is more common in older adults. It means that even in the absence of the clinical diagnosis, many older adults tend to "stock up" on commonly used and preferred items simply because they aren't accustomed to having things like amazon prime and instacart making it easy for them to get what they need fast. Hoarding or "excessive stocking up" can also be a sign of cognitive impairment. Moreover, "collecting" items of interest or perceived as valuable is a fairly common hobby for older adults as well. While the items that they collect may bring them great joy, they can be difficult to store and move from place to place especially when downsizing.

One of the most effective ways to manage the emotions of the downsizing and decluttering process is to keep your care recipient involved in the decision-making. The more in control of the situation they are, the less difficult it will be. It is important to have honest but kind conversations in these situations which takes a certain skill set. You may want to hire a decluttering company that specializes in working with seniors to help you with this process. If they have the training and experience working with the older adult population, they will understand the complexities and approach needed to be successful.

The home itself may be difficult for them to say goodbye to. There are a couple of ways to alleviate some of the stress of this. First, take your time with the move. Walk through each room and ask your care recipient to share stories from living in the home. Ask questions about personal belongings and photos. Sharing their memories and special moments will allow them to feel their emotions related to their belongings. Having the opportunity to feel and process them will help ease the stress.

Second, be sure to set up their new destination with sentimental items that will make them feel at home. You can take a few key pieces of furniture, furnishings, etc. to transform the new space into an abode that feels like home for your care recipient. Plan carefully by taking measurements to ensure the old items will fit in the new space, and be sure to use items that are still in good shape and won't be a hazard to your care recipient. If possible, hang pictures and unpack these special personal items in the new space before your care recipient arrives to ease the shock of the initial transition. The more similar you can make their new setting to their previous home, the better.

When the move is long distance, you may want to consider whether moving them into assisted living versus your home is a better option. This way, if they ultimately need assisted living, they do not have to move more than once. A single move will be easier on everyone rather than multiple moves. Having them closer to you, even in a senior living facility, is ideal because you can check in much more regularly and be actively involved in their care. Regardless of the setting they are moving to, there are some other ways to make the process go more smoothly for a long distance move. To help with the planning, coordination and management of any type of move, you may want to hire a professional. You can use the National Association of Senior Move Managers website as a resource.[30]

THE ADJUSTMENT PERIOD

Moving into a senior living community is a momentous change. Expect that there is going to be a significant adjustment period. Remember to remain empathetic with your care recipient. During this transition period, it is important to validate their concerns and feelings and offer support. If they voice a complaint, attempt to get to the bottom of it. You will want to try and discern what things they just need to get used to and what truly needs to be addressed with management.

When concerns and issues do need to be addressed, I return to the "big 3". Determine which management leader is the most appropriate one to handle the issue- it is best to address it directly with the manager over the area of concern first before taking it to the Administrator. For example, if it is a concern about medication management, talk first with the Director of Nursing. Take note of how they respond? Do you get the support you need? If not, it will be best to escalate it to the Administrator. But going to the Administrator first for every concern is not likely the best approach. Handling concerns within the established hierarchy of the community is going to garner the best results because it is the most efficient way to approach it.

In both assisted living and nursing homes, my top recommendation is always the same. Your active participation in the care of your care recipient makes all the difference. It is important to be visible. Be proactive and get involved in your care recipient's community. Visit often, show interest in getting to know the staff, participate in activities with your care recipient, and if you have the time you may even want to consider volunteering there. The better they know you and your care recipient, the better experience you will ultimately have. You will earn the trust of the staff and they will be more likely to communicate openly with you. Then, when you do have a problem, you are more likely to get the

---

[30] nasmm.org

result you want when you bring it to their attention. It is key to look at the staff and administration of the senior living as partners on the same team as you.

Furthermore, remember that the transition, like any other major life change, is probably going to be difficult. Have patience as your care recipient and the team at the community get accustomed to each other and work out the kinks. You may find your care recipient is well adjusted right away, but you would be in the minority. It could take as long as six months or more for your care recipient to become comfortable in their new surroundings. It is not going to be perfect, but the reasons you decided to make the transition are still true even when faced with challenges. For most who decide to transition to senior living, it is the safest, most appropriate level of care for your care recipient. Instead of questioning your decision, work to find ways to encourage your care recipient and forge a partnership with the community in support of them.

RESISTANCE

It is very common for an older adult to resist when their family or caregiver suggests that they need in-home care, or it is time to consider senior living. One of the hardest first steps is starting the conversation with them about it. If you are feeling anxious about this, you certainly aren't alone. Less than half of older adults have discussed with anyone the potential need for long-term care or how they want to age with their families. If your care recipient is your parent, you want to be careful not to cause your parents to feel "parented." It is common for older adults to feel this way and very hard to avoid. You are likely to be nervous about how they will respond and concerned about changing the dynamic in your relationship. It can certainly be daunting but because proactive planning is the best strategy for long term care planning, putting it off can be extremely detrimental.

In some cases, the care recipient may adamantly refuse and may even become angry or upset. It is easy to write this off as being "stubborn" or "hard-headed." The truth is while reasons vary widely, there are usually a few common themes for the underlying cause behind this type of response. If this happens to you, each objection your care recipient voices should be validated and then you should address them and reassure them. I will explore some of the most common ones so that you can be prepared to face them head on.

Loss of independence. Many older adults are under the false impression that by refusing added care, they are protecting their independence. Of course, it is quite the opposite. Refusing care is actually risking complete loss of independence. If an older adult ends up with an injury because they refuse to accept help, they will inevitably end up in a crisis situation. In a crisis, choices will be much more limited from there on out. It is better to make a decision when you have a choice than to be forced into it during a crisis. One tip is to mention that accepting help in the home is an alternative to assisted living. Many older adults desire to live in their own home as long as possible so allowing professional caregivers to come in may be a preferable option over having to move.

Lack of control. They do not want to give up control and let someone else decide when and how they will receive care. To combat this, involve them in every step of the decision-making process. This allows them to feel empowered and often solidifies their commitment to accepting the assistance.

Desire to retain privacy. Many older adults are concerned about having caregivers in their home or about moving into senior living because they feel they will lose their privacy. Make sure this concern is voiced in the interviews with caregivers or during your senior living tours. Most professional caregivers know how to maintain that fine balance between safety and privacy. If they are aware of this concern, they can use an even more delicate approach with your care recipient.

Embarrassment. This takes the desire for privacy one step further. Sensitive subjects such as incontinence and bathing are likely to cause embarrassment. Counteract this concern immediately by addressing it upfront. By approaching needs like incontinence care and bathing in a straightforward manner with dignity and respect, the awkward feelings your care recipient has will fade to the background.

Fear of becoming a burden. I am here to tell you that most of the time, an older adult does not want to be a burden on friends and loved ones. Ironically, by refusing care, they are often expecting family and friends to pick up the slack and may not even be aware that they are doing so. Sometimes simply letting your care recipient know that accepting help eases your burden is convincing. Your care recipient might be more willing to accept help if they know it gives you peace of mind. Explain your need to reduce your workload, while emphasizing that you want to help them maintain their independence as long as possible.

Denial. Many older adults do not recognize that they need assistance at all. You will be hard pressed to convince them otherwise. They may be offended that you are suggesting they cannot take care of themselves. The best way to handle this is not to insist their own self-care is faltering, which may be true, but to point out how having some help will make things easier on them. For example, you could say something like "I know you can handle all the cleaning and cooking but having some help would give you more time to enjoy hobbies or spending time with your friends".

Start by picking a calm, quiet time when distractions are not likely to interrupt the conversation. Then, open a non-confrontational dialogue with your care recipient. Here are some helpful tactics for starting this conversation:

Don't wait until a crisis. In a crisis situation, decisions can be rushed and tensions can run high. Advance planning is always ideal. Introducing care when things are calm allows for your care recipient to get used to it gradually and on their own terms.

Introduce a less invasive approach first. Ease your care recipient into the idea by suggesting a trial run or respite. A good opportunity may be if you are going away on a business trip, vacation, or preparing for a medical event of your own. This is a good opportunity to suggest that you could use the extra help during that time. Oftentimes once the care recipient tries it out, they decide for themself that having home care is a good thing. Then, once a rapport has been established with a caregiver during the respite period, you may be able to put in place a plan to keep it in place and gradually increase the amount of care over time.

Use someone else as an example. Your care recipient probably has a friend, neighbor, or another family member who is already dealing with some aspect of senior care. Talking about their experience and how they reflect on it, good and bad, can help you gain insight into what they would want for themselves.

Present an article. Use a publication, such as a blog post or journal article, about planning for senior care or long-term care costs as an icebreaker by asking for their thoughts on it.

Put yourself in their shoes. Tell them that you're starting a retirement account or preparing a will for yourself and ask for their input. You can then transition into questions about their plan (or lack thereof).

Focus on Listening. Don't dominate the conversation. Ask open ended questions. What do they want for the future? What worries them? What brings them joy? Let them express their concerns, fears and desires. Be empathetic and validate them. Repeat back to them what you are hearing to show that you are listening and confirm that you heard them right.

Tell them it will help you. Gently explain that you are worried about them, and that having added care can be not only helpful but also enjoyable for them, while providing peace of mind for you.

Provide options to consider. Don't try and force them onto any one particular path. Be open to other ideas even if you already have ideas of your own.

Know when to stop. If you are met with too much resistance from your care recipient, the timing may not be right. Never criticize or argue as this will undermine your progress. Back off and revisit the conversation regularly as the situation and needs change.

At the conclusion of the conversation, attempt to agree upon the next step. For example: "Mom, based on what we discussed today, I am going to start researching quality home care agencies in your area. Are we in agreement?" If the answer is no, take a step back and try something a little less invasive. Repeat until you can find a common ground. Remain empathetic and gentle with your approach, and assure your care recipient that your goal is to follow their lead and focus on their goals. Don't rush them. These decisions are hard and will take time.

Once you have laid the groundwork, you can move forward confidently knowing that you and your care recipient are on the same page and you can start considering the best options for them without wondering if they will be open to the idea. This will make the process much easier for you. Remember to continue revisiting the subject and keep them involved in the process.

While I always encourage a less abrupt, calm approach, you may have tried all of the above and still feel like you are talking to a brick wall. If what I have suggested seems like an impossible task, here are some additional tactics you can try:

Seize an opportunity. The best time to approach your care recipient may be to wait for a topic to come up naturally. For example, when they mention that upkeep of the house is becoming too much to bear.

Try someone else. While it may seem that the one who has been providing most of the care would be the logical choice for the conversation starter, it may be better for someone else to step in so that the relationship between primary caregiver and care recipient can be preserved. If someone else who is not as directly involved in the care has a trusted relationship with the care recipient, the care recipient may be more open to hearing what they have to say.

Try an "intervention". Some families will come together to address this concern "intervention style." This may be a good approach for some, but for others it may come off as confrontational. Consider your care recipient's personality and how they may respond to being approached by several family members at once.

Bring in a professional to help start and guide the conversation. Some older adults respond better to an unrelated third party. Call on your advocacy team—your care recipient may respond best to a particular member of this team, so don't hesitate to leverage that trusted relationship to help you move forward. It can be frustrating that your care recipient would listen to someone else rather than to listen to you, but do not take it personally. Sometimes it takes a direct approach that a professional can more easily facilitate because there are no emotional ties between them. Your care recipient may also view the professional as an expert on the subject and hearing the same things you have said from this third party will confirm that this is the right advice for them.

There are some situations where the situation is truly not safe and it may warrant escalation. This might mean getting help from the Department of Social Services or having their primary physician evaluate competency. If appropriate, you may need to step in and take action using power of attorney in order to ensure your care recipient's safety.

Calling upon my experience a few examples of this that come to mind are:

· When the care recipient has dementia and begins to wander and has the potential to leave the home unattended;

· When the care recipient truly cannot be left alone and there are no resources for in-home care assistance or establishing in-home assistance has been unsuccessful ;

· When a medical condition they have is completely unmanageable such as a diabetic who is unable to check their blood sugars and administer injectable insulin;

· When the care recipient is reckless in their behavior, making them potentially a harm to self or others.

If you are facing any of these challenges, a more drastic action may be necessary if the situation is extremely unsafe. However, I do not suggest tackling it on your own. The best tactic is to immediately involve a third party, such as one of the professionals on your advocacy team, or contact Adult Protective Services and request a social worker to intervene.

TURNING TRAGEDY INTO OPPORTUNITY

Unfortunately, there are times that none of the planning happens before a tragedy strikes. Many people don't even think about senior care while their care recipient is healthy and functional. The truth is, when things are going smoothly, thinking about what could go wrong is unnatural and quite simply falls to the bottom of the priority list.

If you and your care recipient did do pre-planning, when a crisis hits you will be fortunate to use the tools that you put into place to help you make rational rather than emotional decisions. You are fortunate to have a road map which will make your path much easier to navigate. If you find yourself in a crisis situation without having done pre-planning, you can certainly use the unfortunate circumstances to turn a crisis into an opportunity. However, you have no such road map so the dynamics will be drastically different. Try to remain calm and rational because your care recipient will likely be reacting out of fear and not thinking clearly. They will be relying on you to use your best judgment and what you know about them to make decisions in their best interest, even if they don't see it that way at the time. Keep your care recipient's safety and well-being in the forefront and you will be well served.

Usually, the crises are medical in nature and may involve hospitalization. Let me describe for you an example of how you can turn a hospitalization into an opportunity. Let's presume your care recipient has been resistant to hiring caregiver services in the past. As we discussed in an earlier chapter, the hospital discharge planner may suggest that your care recipient relocate to a skilled nursing facility temporarily for rehabilitation. While this recommendation is likely the best plan for their optimal recovery, many older adults simply refuse. This is an opportunity for you. Often when faced with the choice of returning home with in-home care, or going into a skilled nursing facility, they will be willing to do whatever it takes to return home. You can leverage support from the hospital staff (physician, case manager, therapists) to help you convince them that a safe return home would require home care support. It is likely that your care recipient will be much more willing to accept additional support at home if it means they can avoid the skilled nursing facility. You can assure them that the assistance may be temporary, just until they are able to care for themselves as fully as they did before.

Should your care recipient accept going to a skilled nursing facility, there will be additional resources and staff that can help you navigate the process from there. They can assist you with setting up services for when your care recipient does return home. Also, they will have more time to spend with you doing so than the hospital staff. So, use the time your care recipient is in rehab wisely. Do your research into the in-home care agencies, make any necessary changes to the home, and make your support system aware that you will need their help when they come home. Don't wait to "see how it goes." You will undoubtedly need the help, so start assigning those tasks now. It is always better to cancel the support later when you don't need it, than to find yourself needing it and being without.

AGING IN PLACE VS. ASSISTED LIVING

This guide provides a simple comparison of the two options*

Aging in Place	Aging in Place with home care	Assisted Living
Familiar environment and routine	✓	
Convenience: everything in one place	✓	
1:1 care	✓	
Assistance with ADLs	✓	✓
Assistance with IADLs	✓	✓
Housekeeping	LIMITED	✓
Assistance with Medications	LIMITED	✓
Medical oversight	LIMITED	✓
Meals provided	✓	
Easy access to socialization/activities	✓	
All inclusive pricing: no maintenance or upkeep	✓	
Ability to use long term care insurance	✓	✓
Ability to utilize home equity to pay for care	✓	✓
Safe for Dementia	LIMITED	LIMITED
Ability to have pets	✓	LIMITED

*Home care companies and assisted living facilities offer varying services, amenities and pricing structures.

EMERGENCY PLANNING

This checklist will help you plan for emergencies and natural disasters for a care recipient aging in place.

Consider putting together a disaster kit that contains the following:

- Approximately three to five days worth of water, canned or dry food that do not require cooking
- Current Medication List and ample supply of medications
- Copy of health insurance cards
- Medical supplies like syringes
- Copies of all important legal documents
- Copies of identification
- Flashlight and extra batteries
- First aid kit
- Lighters and matches
- Thermal blanket or clothing
- Sleeping bag
- Extra pet supplies if they have pets

Create a list of important contact persons and phone numbers:

- Primary Care Physician
- Medical Specialists (if applicable)
- Medical Agent/Power of Attorney
- Pharmacy
- Local Family or Primary point of contact
- Out of area Primary POC
- Support Persons/Care Providers:
  - > Professional Caregivers
  - > Pet sitter/walker
  - > Housekeeper/maid
  - > Other
- One or two neighbors

- Utility Companies
  - Electric
  - Water/Sewer
  - Gas
  - Other
- Pet's Veterinarian (if applicable)

MULTIGENERATIONAL LIVING

This guide will aid you in considering multi-generational living.

Consider Beforehand:

- Where in the home is the ideal space for them to move into? Do you have a separate living space, or will they share all of the same living spaces with you?
- Will it be necessary to make renovations or physical accommodations to the home?
- What are the potential safety concerns that need to be considered?
- How will their presence in the home affect your daily routine and schedule?
- What are the financial implications of bringing them into the home?
- Do you and your care recipient fight/disagree often? Can you have open discussions about your feelings with one another?
- Do they smoke or drink, and if so will you allow this in your home?
- Do they have any pets to bring along? If so, how will they get along with your pet(s)?
- How will this arrangement affect the other family relationships (spouse, children, etc.)?

Discuss Openly:

- Will they be expected to contribute, financially or otherwise to the household?
- Will you be compensated now or later for providing this support? Will other family members contribute and if so, how?
- Will they participate in all or some of the family activities/meals/etc.?
- How will privacy and independence be maintained?
- Will they need help with their personal care, hygiene, etc.?
- What will they bring with them? (such as furniture and other large items).
- Discuss whether in-home care will be necessary, and how it will be paid for.

- Will they be expected to contribute, financially or otherwise to the household?
- What will their role be in caring for children (if applicable)?
- Address fears, concerns, expectations of all parties involved. Talk through your emotions and be supportive of one another
- Give consideration to the logistics of the move itself and make a plan for the first few weeks after the move. Who will do what?

RED FLAGS

Use this guide to help you identify red flags which may indicate that your care recipient is in need of more care*

- Forgetting to put on glasses or hearing aids
- Drastic/sudden weight gain or loss
- Difficulty with mobility (for example, having a hard time getting up and out of a chair)
- Uncleanliness or household tasks going unattended
- Frequent falls (more than 1 in 6 months)
- Being unkempt or inappropriately dressed for the weather or occasion
- Insufficient personal hygiene
- Difficulty managing medications
- Stacks of mail or mail piling up in the mailbox
- Unpaid bills, debt collectors calling or bounced checks
- Lack of food or spoiled food in the home
- Pets are being neglected
- Medications not filled or out of date
- Frequent driving incidents
- Lack of socialization
- Safety hazards, such as leaving the stove or iron on and walking away

*If you do notice some of these signs the best action to take is to discuss your concerns with your care recipient and potential next steps.

HOME CARE AGENCY INTERVIEW

This checklist will help you when you interview home care agencies.

- How long has the agency been in business?
- Who are the owners of the company? Why did they open the company?
- How do they select and train their employees?
- Are the caregivers they employ legal employees or independent contractors?
- What type of background checks do they perform?
- Do they provide their employees with benefits?
- What insurance policies do they have (malpractice, worker's comp, etc.)
- How are call-offs handled?
- What procedures are in place to handle off hours emergencies?
- What is their policy related to employee theft or abuse?
- Does a licensed nurse oversee the services? Do they provide support in the home?
- How often are care needs assessed? What is involved with plan of care changes?
- Ask what the agency's policy is on changing out a caregiver if it isn't a good match.
- If you have long term care insurance, how do they handle claims?
- Ask for written information on:
  - > Billing policies and procedures
  - > Policies related to confidentiality
  - > Policies and procedures related to handling complaints

CHOOSING A SENIOR LIVING

This checklist will help you when touring senior living facilities.

- Are you welcomed warmly? How long does it take for someone to help you?
- Ask how long has the facility been in business?
- Ask about the owners of the facility. How long have they owned it?
- Ask if they are required to have a state license? If so, what state agency governs them?
- Ask for a copy of their most recent state survey (if applicable)
- Observe staff and residents engaging with each other and take note of their interactions
- Ask for a copy of the activity schedule. Take note: are the scheduled activities happening?
- Ask for a sample menu. Better yet, ask to participate in a meal
- Observe the cleanliness of the facility. Take notice of any unpleasant odors
- Take note of the building's layout and design features
- Is the facility well kept? Well lighted? In good repair?
- Ask to see the exact suite that is available for your care recipient to rent, if possible
- Be sure to ask to see any outside recreation areas
- Ask if they provide transportation services and learn about the options available
- Ask what services are provided on site
- Take notice or or ask what security measures they have in place
- Find out if a nurse is on duty or on call 24/7
- Ask what doctors and other healthcare professionals are contracted with the facility
- Ask what hospital they use for emergencies
- Find out about staffing ratios on all shifts
- If it is a secure dementia facility, ask what security system do they use, and what procedures do they use to ensure the safety of the

residents?

· Ask about their financial policies

· Ask about how they handle complaints

· Ask about their move out policies

· Ask what they will do if there comes a time they cannot meet your care recipient's needs

Interview Questions for the "Big 3" (Executive Director, the Director of Nursing, and the Director of Dining Services).

· How long have they been working there?

· What is their professional background?

· What made them choose to work there?

· What do they like about the company they work for? What do they not like?

· What do they think makes their facility better than the competition?

NOTES

CHAPTER 4

THE SOCIAL

You have two hands. One to help yourself, and one to help others.
- Audrey Hepburn

RISKS OF ISOLATION IN THE ELDERLY

Aging can be very isolating and lonely, which can have many damaging effects. The social aspects of long-term care are infrequently considered by older adults. We know social connections are vital for positive physical and mental health. But as we age, friends begin to pass away and they may begin to forget to reach out to friends. Opportunities for social interaction lessen dramatically and social networks tend to deteriorate. This is likely one of the primary reasons that depression is so common in older adults. Unfortunately, depression is often overlooked or misdiagnosed. Like dementia, while common, it is not "normal". Also similar to dementia, it is stigmatized and not talked about much. It is important to remember that depression is a medical condition, and it is not the patient's "fault" that they are experiencing it.

The symptoms of depression can overlap or mimic other conditions, such as dementia. For example, they may become socially withdrawn, irritable, or fatigued. They may also experience extreme weight gain or weight loss. To complicate things further, depression is even more common in people with a dementia diagnosis. If you suspect your care recipient is experiencing depression, you should talk to them about it. Most people, older adults included, will need either medication, therapy, or a combination to overcome symptoms of depression. It is not something to be ignored or taken lightly. Depression can lead to serious health problems, and even increases the risk of death by suicide.[31] Therefore, it is imperative to bring any concern about depression to your care recipient's medical provider's attention.

There are many ways to increase the level of socialization your care recipient enjoys. This involves the prioritization and encouragement of trusted, interpersonal relationships, a combination of family, friends, community, and professional. Begin by increasing your own contact with them. In the past you may not have gotten together as often. Many families only gather on holidays and major events. Increasing this frequency even slightly can make a drastic impact on their mental health.

I recognize this is easier said than done and I do not mean to diminish this challenge. Even one extra stop each week can be extremely burdensome on an already overloaded schedule, especially for the Sandwich Generation caregiver. And of course for long distance caregivers, this is almost impossible. Later in this section we will talk more about the additional complexities of caregiving from afar. But, even from a distance, consider that perhaps you usually call once or twice a month now. Adding one more call, particularly if you schedule it and block out the time, may not be too burdensome. You can also help them stay in touch with their existing network by reminding them to call, sending birthday and holiday cards on their behalf, or helping them use social media to stay connected with friends and family. Reach out and invite friends and family to visit and help facilitate these interactions.

Being able to drive gives older adults independence and access to the lifeline

---

[31] who.int/news-room/fact-sheets/detail/depression

of their social network. But, there comes a point for many care recits that it is no longer safe to get behind the wheel. When this happens, they are at an increased risk of the detriments of isolation. In this instance, find ways to ensure your care recipient still gets out to enjoy activities they love. For example, if your care recipient routinely attended faith programs, community events, or volunteered, it is very likely that they will want to continue to do so even when they can no longer drive. The good news is, the organization they were involved with wants them to also. So, reach out to the leaders of the organizations they were tied to and have them help. Many will even have members who are willing to pick up and bring others along with them. Furthermore, local senior centers and adult day programs often have vans or buses that they can use to transport local participants desiring to come to the center. Many communities have these types of centers designed to provide aging community members the ability to stay social and active and connected with others. They offer an array of different events and usually provide meals which also helps ensure your care recipient continues to eat healthy.

Another risk of social isolation in older adults is susceptibility to fraud and abuse. As your care recipient gets older they become lonely, and they also become vulnerable. This happens because to combat loneliness, they may fall victim to phone solicitations and door knockers. In seeking personal connection, they may inadvertently welcome those who have sinister intentions.

Fortunately, communities are designed with many pillars that can support and protect older adults, such as law enforcement, health care, faith centers, banks, schools, and community centers. Tapping into these pillars are a vital way to protect against this type of predatory activity. Most will be more than willing to help you keep an eye on your care recipient, and keep you informed if they have any concerns.

Another strategy to combat social isolation is to utilize in-home care. The in-home care company may be able to provide transportation to and from desired community activities. Furthermore, many home care companies offer "friendly visits" for those who are homebound which are designed to be less medical in nature and puts the focus on social engagement. The "caregivers" are frequently individuals who have training and experience in fields such as recreational therapy, occupational therapy, social work, or related fields. This type of service is also offered by many nonprofits, although the visitors are usually volunteers and not necessarily skilled individuals. In utilizing this option, it can be very helpful to your care recipient's caregiver to help them connect with them by providing insight into their likes and dislikes, hobbies, interests and background. The caregiver may be able to use this information to cater their activities in a way that your care recipient will enjoy, and possibly find a common thread with them earlier on that will allow them to bond. Providing this to the in-home care agency upfront may help them to better match a caregiver that will have some commonalities with your care recipient.

One primary reason people choose assisted living over keeping their care recipient at home is the socialization factor. Choosing to place your care recipient in a senior living community can decrease these risks but not eliminate them entirely, as many older adults in senior living communities are socially withdrawn as well. This is why the activities programs we talked about in chapter three are so important in senior living.

DRIVING

I mentioned the fact that many older adults lose their ability to drive safely in the previous section. I wanted to take a moment to explore this, because it comes up ALL the time, and can be one of the biggest stressors on the relationship of a caregiver and care recipient. My own grandmother drove her car through her front porch. Thankfully she was not seriously injured but this was a big eye opener for my family. So, when I get asked about this I always think of her and the risks that continuing to drive, especially with cognitive impairments, can impose.

I will begin by stating I don't believe there should be a blanket rule or "cut-off age" for a driver's license, as all people age differently. I know some people in their 90s who are perfectly capable of driving, perhaps better than their younger counterparts. But, let's face it, the natural changes of aging do tend to impede safe driving, such as decreased vision, hearing, and even mobility. Fortunately, many of these changes we can compensate for, such as with adjustable seat cushions.

There are some things we can't compensate for, such as decreased judgment, concentration and reaction time. As we age, it does take longer to think through an idea and react, and it can be harder to concentrate and do more than one thing at a time, which is necessary for driving safely. For those with dementia, or chronic illnesses who are on many medications, this may be even worse for them.

If you have concerns that your care recipient should not be driving anymore, there are varying solutions for this problem. In some geographical locales, there are more resources than others. California, for example, has a Senior Driver Ombudsman program which is sponsored by the Department of Motor Vehicles. It is designed to represent the interest of public safety for all residents, while ensuring that older drivers are treated with the dignity and respect they deserve.

Nationally there are also resources such as the "Car Fit" classes through AARP and AAA, which is an educational community-based program that promotes safe driving by focusing on safety, comfort and fit.[32] At these events, older drivers are given practical information on easy ways to accommodate the natural changes of aging. Plus, older adults may qualify for a discount on their car insurance if they take the class. There are also driving improvement courses for senior drivers offered by AAA both in person and online.[33]

Many occupational therapists are certified in driver safety, and can evaluate your care recipient with a quick behind-the-wheel test. You can also contact a rehabilitation clinic to see if they offer a "senior behind-the-wheel" program. During such a program, the OT will offer a clinical assessment and make recommendations. If your care recipient passes the test, great. You can rest more easily with them behind the wheel. If not, the OT can be the "bad guy," so to speak, removing that burden from you. The American Occupational Therapy Association website offers a wealth of information on this topic, and you can

[32] car-fit.org

[33] exchange.aaa.com/safety/senior-driver-safety-mobility/aaa-roadwise-driver/

[34] aota.org/practice/practice-settings/driving-community-mobility/driving-practitioner-directory

even locate a safe driving specialist through the search function on the site.[34]

Sometimes the process of getting your care recipient to give up driving can take a while. It is one of those markers of independence that aging adults are very hesitant to give up. But, driving is a privilege, not a right, and we must always consider the safety of others on the road. If the situation is extremely risky and you cannot take the time to address it in steps, I suggest talking to your care recipient's physician. Sometimes they can help deliver the news in a way that your care recipient will comply. For example, perhaps they can say that they should not drive while taking their prescribed medication.

If that does not work, take the keys. It sounds harsh, but it is the safest thing to do. FIrst of course make sure that the person still has a reliable means of transportation to medical appointments and other important outings, whether it be public transportation, Uber or Lyft, or a senior transportation service.

PETS

Another excellent way to avoid isolation is through the joyful companionship of a pet. There are great mental health benefits to pet ownership. A pet can instill a sense of pride and responsibility that is good for the psyche of an older adult. The presence of an animal can be extremely comforting, and it also may provide an added sense of security.[35]

When my father in law passed away, he left behind his beloved dog Snuffy who we have now adopted. Caring for Snuffy was a delight for him, it gave him a sense of purpose and fulfillment. The joy that Snuffy gave him was apparent, and I know he was grateful for the companionship and love the dog offered him. Unfortunately, as my father in law's health declined, he was not as capable to keep up with the demands of caring for a dog and certain tasks became burdensome, such as walking Snuffy, particularly in the heat of the summer months.

Having a pet generally keeps people more physically active and healthier. Although, it is true that some older adults may have more difficulty keeping up

---

[35] newsinhealth.nih.gov/2018/02/power-pets

with the physical demands of caring for a pet. Fortunately, there are some easy ways to avoid pet care taking a toll on your care recipient's well-being. The following are some steps you can take:

- Get pet supplies automatically shipped to the home through an online service.
- Get products such as automatic water and food bowls to reduce the frequency of the need to bend and refill bowls. For cats, there are also self cleaning litter boxes.
- Hire a dog walker when the daily walks become too burdensome.
- Hire a vet that offers house call services. You can find a groomer that does this too.

If your care recipient would benefit from having a pet, consider adopting a senior pet instead of a puppy or kitten. A younger pet's needs may be too demanding. There are some programs that match senior pets with older adult owners and usually offer reduced adoption fees. However it is important to recognize that in some cases, older pets may have health conditions that are a challenge to care for. Furthermore, make sure that the pet is spayed or neutered to avoid having a litter of pups or kittens underfoot.

If your care recipient is having a hard time caring for their pet from a financial aspect, utilize local resources to support them. There are charities such as the Humane Society that have programs to assist with payment for services such as grooming, dental care and temporary boarding. There is also a grant through the Meals on Wheels program that helps homebound older adults by delivering pet supplies to their homes.

Finally, if your care recipient lives in a senior living community look into pet therapy programs. Many senior living facilities have volunteers or partners with local organizations that will bring in therapy dogs to provide emotional support to their residents.

LONG-DISTANCE CAREGIVING

It has become extremely common for families to be scattered geographically.

Education or vocational opportunities, romantic relationships, military connections, or simply lifestyle preferences are amongst the many reasons for adult children to leave their hometown to build their lives elsewhere. When the need arises, many of them do not wish to uproot themselves from the place they now call home to return to their hometown and care for an aging family member. Moreover, many older adults are hesitant to leave the comfort of the communities they call home, even once their independence begins to falter. According to a recent survey conducted by AARP, only 29 percent of older adults say they are willing to relocate to another community.[36]

If they are not willing to move, and you are not able or willing to relocate to where they are, multigenerational living may not be a feasible solution for your family. The National Institute on Aging defines long-distance caregiving as living more than an hour drive away from your care recipient.[37] You may even live far enough away that a plane ride is necessary. This adds a layer of complexity to your situation as you must manage their affairs from afar. There are two of my top five tips that stand out as most important for long-distance caregivers: "G"-- Get organized and "S"-- Seek support. I will expand on why these are so important for long distance caregivers in particular. But first, let's discuss how the use of technology can be beneficial in long distance caregiving.

It is true that long distance caregivers can manage a lot of tasks remotely, using modern technology and the internet. Communication technology like Zoom, Facetime and Skype have made it easier to keep caregivers and care recipients connected. Phone calls are nice but being able to see them on video will give you a much greater sense of comfort. Furthermore, you will be better able to assess whether what they are telling you is true than you can with a phone call. And your care recipient will also enjoy seeing your smiling face!

There are an array of other technologies available to increase safety and independence of your care recipient, giving you added peace of mind. There are home monitoring systems, medication reminder devices, even robots! Many caregivers have also found ways to use Alexa, Dot, Google Home and the

---

[36] Where We Live, Where We Age: Trends in Home and Community Preferences by Joanne Binette, AARP Research, November 2021 Home and Community Preferences Survey
[37] CAREGIVING IN THE U.S. 2020

like to make their caregiving experiences easier. I am not making a product endorsement, but in my research ElliQ is one of the most comprehensive products I have found, from helping your care recipient read and respond to messages, to making appointments, providing daily affirmations, and reminding them about medications.[38]

The technological advances in the senior caregiving space have made a tremendously positive impact, but it will only take us so far. Inevitably, you are going to have to make in person trips to support your care recipient. This is why getting organized should be a high priority for long-distance caregivers. When you visit, you are going to need to pack a lot into a short time, especially if they are few and far between. You will need to be as intentional with your time as possible; you won't want to spend all of your time rummaging through your care recipient's home for the things you need when you visit, and leave no time for enjoyment of one another's company. Leaving plenty of time for personal connection with your care recipient is vital to ensure they are refreshed socially and emotionally by your visit.

When possible, schedule important medical, financial and legal appointments when you can be physically present for them. Virtual options are great for squeezing less important meetings in between, but there is nothing like being face to face with paper and pen for these critical meetings. This means bring ready with what you need to have to present to the professional you are meeting with and any questions prepared to make the most of the allotted time. Don't forget to use the doctor's visit checklist I provided in chapter two.

Seeking support is fairly obvious in its importance. As a long-distance caregiver, understand that you will be at a clear disadvantage not being able to monitor things with your own eyes. So much can slip through the cracks when you are relying on your care recipient's report and not able to see things for yourself. Decline can happen gradually and it may not be obvious to you over the phone or even a virtual check in. Remember when I introduced the idea of the advocacy team in chapter one? In long distance caregiving, I cannot stress enough the importance of identifying those people that you can rely on to

---

[38] elliq.com

provide the "boots on the ground" support that your care recipient will need. You will rely heavily on this advocacy team to be your eyes and ears, and advocate for your care recipient when you cannot. Regular check-ins by the local support system will keep you apprised of little changes that may be of concern.

If it becomes apparent that your care recipient cannot live alone and is insistent on staying in their community, you are going to have a much more difficult time than caregivers who live in close proximity to their care recipient. It is also likely to require more in terms of financial resources to support them. Without local informal caregivers to fill in the gaps, professional caregiving hours will add up quickly. You will also spend more in travel expenses going back and forth to deal with crises as they arise. At a minimum, if your care recipient lives in a rural area you may want to try and convince them to move closer to or within a larger city if possible. This will afford them more care options, bring them closer to hospitals and medical offices, and make travel easier for you.

Since aging in place will undoubtedly be more challenging to manage from a distance, you may want to look into senior living facilities in their area. We are going to talk about Senior Living options in a later section. Senior Living may be the best solution from a social standpoint as well, since you are not near to act as a catalyst with their support system, keeping it engaged and active. However, caring from afar, even when your care recipient is in senior living, is no piece of cake. In fact, it can be increasingly frustrating as your care recipient declines and you become fully reliant on the staff of the senior living facility to be your eyes and ears. It may be even more beneficial to engage an Aging Life care manager or other senior advocate in this instance. Having this type of advocate to serve as the mediator between the family and the professional staff can make things much easier.

When it comes to long-distance caregiving I must also touch on something known as "snow-birding". Snow-birding is unique to certain locales and we see a lot of it here in the Washington DC Metro area. What it means is when an individual or a couple, usually upon retirement, will decide to split their time between one location and another, generally going to a warmer location during the winter months and a colder location during the summer months. This structure is more challenging for caregivers when their care recipient needs their support, because inadvertently they have almost doubled the work. You will need to keep up with two medical systems, two sets of doctors and other professionals, two sets of household bills and maintenance services, and the list goes on! The task of organizing care and services for your care recipient is difficult in one location, much less two. But, if this is the lifestyle your care recipient is committed to living, as with most scenarios there are ways you can prepare in advance to make this arrangement easier in the long term. I have put together a guide for long distance caregiving for this chapter. I will finalize my thoughts on this subject with this tip- be sure to prioritize what is most important to accomplish on each visit and tackle those things first. Lower priority items can wait, so don't stress yourself out trying to get it all done and miss out on precious time with your care recipient!

SELF-ACTUALIZATION IN AGING

We have covered Maslow's hierarchy and the deficiency needs that we as caregivers and advocates are responsible for meeting for our care recipient. However, imagine if we as a society could slow down and attempt to meet the growth needs in aging as well. Don't assume that your care recipient cannot or does not want or need personal development just because they are of advanced age. Many older adults find immense fulfillment in doing things like taking a college course, attending conferences or serving on an advisory committee. Older adults have more time available to them, they sometimes just need the encouragement or the connection to the right outlets to get them on the path of enjoying self-actualizing activities in their elder years. They have (hopefully) led enriching lives building their skills, talents and capabilities and for many, the slowing down or stopping of this in advanced age can be very devaluing. In Geriatrician Dr. Williams Thomas's book, "What are Old People Good For?" he ardently champions viewing our older adult years as a growth stage of life. Dr. Thomas founded the groundbreaking Eden Alternative® and Green Houses® initiatives. Through these projects he provides some ways that long term care facilities in particular can apply these principles to greatly impact their resident's quality of life and sense of purpose.

The lack of appreciation in the United States for the knowledge and expertise older adults possess saddens me to no end. Our society places high value on youth, and tends to dismiss aging adults, treating them as if they have nothing to contribute. Families tend to get so occupied with what the kids are doing that they forget to pay attention to what their elders have to share. They raised children, ran households, built companies, faced challenges and overcame adversity. They have a lot they can teach the younger generation. Unfortunately, because this is so undervalued, many older people do not bother to share stories or advice with the younger people in their lives. This untapped information dies with them. Who knows what impact it could have made if it had been shared? One way we can strive to help older adults meet their personal growth needs is by sharing what they know. When an older adult has an outlet to teach and share what they have learned with others, it can be life-changing for both the giver and the receiver. Consider trying to find a young person for your care recipient to mentor. It is likely that your care recipient has knowledge and experience that they can share that would be helpful to someone getting started in life or their career. You can reach out to schools, civic or volunteer organizations to locate young people in the community who might be interested in such mentorship opportunities.

I strongly urge you to encourage your care recipient to document their experiences for you and others in some form. When I worked in the estate planning law firm, the attorney referred to this chronicling of life stories and the wisdom gained from them for their heirs as an Ethical Will. The emphasis on the emotional and spiritual side of estate planning was one of the reasons I was attracted to working at this particular firm. If you are interested you can read more about this approach in the book he co-authored, which I will reference in the index. In my experience, most people neglect to pass on the non-tangible but priceless heirlooms such as memories and sound advice. What they fail to recognize is that frequently their loved ones would prefer these things over the material items and money. My primary recommendation is to not wait until it is too late. You can do this in any number of ways. One option is to have them write it down. This may be challenging for older adults if they have any physical debility in their hands. But remember, they may have already done it. Ask your care recipient if they ever journaled or wrote down stories. You may be able to locate and revisit these journals with them. You can read them together, ask questions, and bond over their memories. You can also use photo albums to do this. Flip through the photos and ask questions about them.

You can also write it down for them as they verbally share stories from their past with you or record a video or audio of them speaking. Ask them about the most pivotal moments in their life. Get specific with your questions. Just asking "tell me about your life" may not be enough to open them up. Try instead something like "Mom, what was the most challenging thing about raising 5 kids under 10?" or "Dad, what inspired you to start your own business?". By asking something specific, you are more likely to jog their memories and get them to answer you in a more meaningful way.

Finally, remember that not all people are social butterflies. If your care recipient was never social, don't try and force it on them now. Some older adults are perfectly happy living their private lives with visits only from close family and friends. In my time working in nursing homes and assisted living, this was one thing that I always struggled with. The regulators of these facilities want to see "engaged, active residents" (and so do the families). During their visits, they are looking for full activities schedules and they want to see residents participating. I understand the value of this of course, and we need to ensure enough active engagement is available for those who want it. But, not all residents wish to participate. When we would receive feedback from a regulator that we needed to work on a particular resident's activity level I would first consider what this resident's personality and history were like. If they were never a social person, I was not going to try and change their habits. It is important to remember that your care recipient has an individual personality and preferences and we should always be honoring them to the best of our abilities.

INFANTILIZING OLDER ADULTS

The final topic I want to touch on in this chapter is one that is a pet peeve of mine. I spoke earlier in this book about the ageism that is frequently found in the medical community. It isn't just in the medical community, it is everywhere. We, as caregivers, advocates and quite simply as human beings need to act in such a way that contributes to the reduction of this ageism. One of the primary ways we can do this is by treating older adults with the respect they deserve, in private and in public. Respect for elders is a common edict regardless of what culture or religion one belongs to, but unfortunately in my career I have seen the opposite of that reflected consistently, across the board.

I am not suggesting you become a fierce crusader for elder rights. If that is your calling, by all means, have at it! However, there is one simple way that we can all make a great impact. In our interactions with older adults (our care recipient and others we encounter) remember that they are not children, and should not be talked to that way. Doing so is denying them the dignity and respect that they deserve.

Most importantly, do not talk down to them or change the tone of your voice as you might with a child or even a pet. This is not appropriate. Furthermore, refrain from using terms of endearment or "pet names". For instance, don't call someone who is not your grandmother "Grandma", or refer to an older adult as "darling" "honey" or "sweetie". Start with Mr./Mrs. followed by their last name. If they give you permission to use their first name, or even a nickname, oblige their request. Otherwise, continue addressing them formally.

I also urge you to not ignore older people in social settings. If you are sitting in the lobby of a medical office waiting on your care recipient, make small talk with the older adults around you. Engage in a light-hearted conversation that you might with someone your own age. Often older adults are ignored in social situations, but they too enjoy small talk. Older people have lived more life than you, and you may be able to identify a valuable connection with them.

Remember, hearing problems are common amongst older adults but you can increase the likelihood of being understood by slowing down, enunciating, making eye contact and ensuring that the older person can clearly see your lips move. Of course you want to speak loudly enough to be heard, but you do not have to yell. Yelling adds to the feeling of being spoken down to.

Perhaps most importantly, when a conversation is being had *about* your care recipient (such as with their physician, therapist, or attorney) do not speak for them or over them. Ask for and validate their input. Allow them ample time to ask questions. I refer to this point in several places in the book– I bring it up multiple times because it is so important to remember. Apply the golden rule in all of these situations, consider how you want to be treated and treat your care recipient and other older adults accordingly.

LONG DISTANCE CAREGIVING

This guide includes suggestions which will aid you in caring for an older adult from a distance, or for "snow-birds".

- Encourage them to use a national bank, pharmacy, etc. (this way, there will likely be an accessible branch near them and also near you)
- Set up online accounts for everything (all bills, services, vendors, etc.) and keep a list of the websites and passwords; this will allow you to quickly gain access in an emergency
  - Most healthcare systems have an online portal for medical records, labs, test results, etc.
- Ensure that they always keep up with prescription refills, but don't use a mail order system (this will avoid any issues with the medications going to the wrong place when they are visiting you or their other residence)
- It could be easier to use Original Medicare and a national supplement that can be utilized wherever they are nationally, as opposed to any local or regional plans*
- Help them embrace technology within their comfort level (staying connected is much easier with technology)
- Estate planning: using a Living Trust vs. a Last Will and Testament can make handling their estate when they pass much easier on the Trustee/Executor**
- Understand their legal residency status
  - There is a difference between "domicile" and "residency"; "domicile" refers to a taxpayer's primary and permanent home (a taxpayer can only have one, which is considered for estate tax purposes), while a taxpayer can have more than one "residence" if they have homes in more than one state.
- Enlist an advocate- ask someone local to help you keep an eye on your care recipient and alert you of any concerns (this could be someone such as a friend, neighbor, or member of their church, or, you could hire an Aging Life Care Manager)

*Consult with a qualified Medicare consultant for personalized guidance.
**Consult with an estate planning attorney for personalized guidance.

NOTES

CHAPTER 5

*Money can't buy happiness, but it will certainly get you
a better class of memories.*
-Ronald Reagan

As already noted, many older adults will need day-to-day assistance in order to age in place successfully.[39] Knowing how likely this is, one of the most important questions you can ask yourself is "How will my care recipient pay for care"? And the sooner you ask it, the better! Most people wait until it is too late. I did not save this category for last because it is the least important. In fact, many decisions you will have to make that we already discussed will be reliant on the resources available. In this chapter we will explore further the impact that financial restraints can have on your planning. I saved this category for last because you may need to tackle it first, and it will be fresh on your mind as you get started!

---

[39] Long-Term Services and Supports for Older Americans: Risks and Financing Research Brief Jun 30, 2015 Revised February 2016 by Melissa Favreault, Urban Institute and Judith Dey, Office of the Assistant Secretary for Planning and Evaluation

President Reagan said it best with his quote: "Money can't buy happiness, but it will certainly get you a better class of memories." I am not sure when the Great Communicator made this statement, but when he did he probably did not anticipate he would be diagnosed with Alzheimer's disease shortly following his presidency and live for another ten years with it. It is true that having more money equates to more options, and therefore a better class of memories (particularly for one's family) in the final stage of life. The better your care recipient saved for their retirement years, the easier it will be to secure quality long-term care services when they are needed.

Long-term care can be one of life's most burdensome expenses. It isn't the cost of home care or assisted living alone. The little things add up: equipment, medications, medical supplies, adult diapers, and more. The cost of care is staggering, especially when they are unexpected and not well planned for. Fortunately for President Reagan, he had both a supportive spouse and sufficient resources. However, even if your care recipient's resources are limited, there are still options.

Knowing what you are working with from a financial aspect and planning ahead will increase the options available and avoid disappointments later. Remember the "U" in the GUESS acronym- understand your care recipient. This does not only mean medically but financially as well. It is best to gain a full understanding of your care recipient's resources, assets and liabilities well before a need for long-term care arises. However, we will come back to the U. First, let's shift gears and focus on the E. That's right, education! Here in the United States, the public payor sources for healthcare are Medicare and Medicaid. Many older adults and their caregivers are confused about what Medicare and Medicaid are, and there are also a lot of misconceptions out there. So I want to start this chapter by clearing up some of this confusion first.

MEDICARE AND MEDICAID

A common false impression is that Medicare and Medicaid will cover all long-term care expenses when they are needed. The truth is far from it. Medicare and Medicaid are not complete sources for funding long term care. Therefore, your care recipient should not rely on these sources to pay for their long-term care.

190

Understanding they are and what services they will and will not pay for is a good first step.

Let's start with Medicare. Medicare is government-funded medical insurance available to people who are over age 65, and some people under 65 with certain disabilities and medical conditions. It is important to recognize that Medicare coverage is intermittent, temporary, and incomplete when it comes to long term care. It often comes as a shock to older adults to discover that the long-term care services they need, even if medically necessary, are not covered by Medicare. One can expect Medicare to kick in to cover some long term care costs, but far from all. I have put together a guide that outlines the basics of what you can expect Medicare to cover, and this chapter provides a basic overview, but understand that this is not individualized advice. Fully understanding how Medicare does factor into your plan can only come from individualized advice, so be sure to tap into your advocacy team resources for education and support in this area.

MEDICARE ALPHABET SOUP

Original Medicare has 2 parts: Part A and Part B. Part A is hospital insurance and is available to you with no out-of-pocket premiums if either you or your spouse paid into Medicare through payroll taxes for at least 40 quarters. While there are no premiums, there are annual deductibles and copays. If you did not pay into Medicare for the minimum number of quarters, you can still purchase Medicare Part A for a monthly premium. You can expect that Part A will cover inpatient hospital care, rehabilitative (short-term care) in a skilled nursing facility under certain requirements, home health care and hospice care under certain conditions.

Part B is outpatient insurance. It is Part B that covers doctor's care, preventive and screening services, some medical supplies and equipment and outpatient services. Unlike Part A, Part B does come with a monthly premium, as well as annual deductibles and copays. While there is a standard B premium, you may pay more if your adjusted gross income is over a set amount. This

---

[40] medicare.gov

adjustment is called income-related monthly adjustment amount, or "IRMAA".[40] You can contact Social Security to find out what your estimated premium will be. It is also important to note that if someone does not enroll in Part B when they first become eligible, there may end up being a penalty. I will explain more about enrollment penalties later.

In addition to Parts A and B, you will need to be aware of Part D. Part D is prescription drug coverage as an optional add-on that requires monthly premiums, annual deductibles and copays. Your care recipient will need to enroll in an approved plan and be covered under both Medicare Parts A and B. IRMAA applies to part D as well. Part D is so important because the costs of medications can be extremely burdensome for many older adults.

Part D by law is available to all persons who qualify for Medicare, but it is provided by third parties so you must shop around for a plan that works for you. Since the drugs that are covered by any particular Part D plan can change from year to year, you will want to review Part D coverage annually. Use your care recipient's current medication list, and look for the specific drugs you need coverage for on the plan's formulary. Part of my responsibilities when I worked in a nursing facility was to review new potential resident's medication lists and determine the costs of the drugs they took. The reason this was my responsibility was because during the rehabilitation stay at a nursing facility, the facility was responsible for providing the drugs the patient required while there. This meant that the costs of those drugs came out of the facility's bottom line. I was partially tasked with keeping this financial burden to a minimum, by either denying admission to patients whose medication costs were too high, or requesting that the patient be switched to another medication prior to admission to the facility, when possible. Because I had this responsibility, I was acutely aware of the astronomical costs of some medications that older adults take routinely.

I once encountered a resident in the nursing facility who was prescribed an injectable medication she needed for her osteoporosis. The drug cost over $3,000.00 per month. Since this was a new medication she had started in the hospital, I asked if she would need to continue it and if there were any less expensive alternatives. The answers to those questions were yes and no, respectively. At the time it was the only medication the doctor deemed appropriate for her condition. I suggested to the daughter upon admission that she look into her insurance coverage for the injection. She did, and unfortunately, it was not covered under her Part D plan. This was a shock and a painful burden for this resident, at least until she was able to enroll in a new plan that would cover the drug. This is only one example, I encountered situations like this one all the time. Therefore, I cannot stress to you how important ensuring that your care recipient is enrolled in Part D and has a plan that is appropriate for their needs.

We talked about Parts A and B, and then we covered Part D. You might be wondering what happened to C? Part C is a little harder to explain. An alternative to Original Medicare is a Medicare Advantage plan. These plans are known as Part C, and they are bundled plans which must cover the same emergency services and most of the same medical services as Original Medicare. They usually also include Part D (prescription). These plans are contracted by private insurance companies, but they must follow the same rules as Medicare. They are usually more affordable premium-wise, and often will cover things like vision, dental and hearing, which Original Medicare does not. The types of Medicare Advantage plans available vary in different areas. They also set annual limits for out-of-pocket costs, which help enrollees budget for out-of-pocket expenses. This can be an attractive option to enrollees. However, many people purchase a Medicare Advantage plan based on promised benefits that sound attractive at first but wind up being unnecessary, and find themselves without coverage for needed services. This is a primary disadvantage that I have seen. For example, frequently during my time working in a skilled nursing facility in the Admissions department, I would encounter situations where a prospective resident for a short-term rehabilitative stay would contact our facility, and state that they had Medicare to be the payor for their stay. A primary function of my role at the facility was to review the hospital records to determine if our facility was a good fit for the patient (in other words, could we meet their needs and did they have an appropriate payor source). What I would learn once the hospital sent over their records was that they had a Medicare Advantage plan, not

Original Medicare. My next step was to verify the plan's benefits and eligibility. It was common for these plans to require a copayment starting much sooner than with Original Medicare. Original Medicare covers skilled nursing facilities for rehabilitative care at 100 percent for up to 20 days following a qualifying inpatient hospital stay. On day 21, a co-payment would be applied which at that time was a little under $130.00 per day. If the resident had a Medicare supplement plan this would usually cover this co-payment. However the Medicare Advantage plans would often have a co-payment starting for example on day one or day three. This would come as a shock to the potential resident and often cause a problem if they were unable to afford the co-payment. It could throw their entire hospital discharge plan into a tailspin.

Furthermore, Medicare Advantage plans do not work exactly the same way as Original Medicare. As I mentioned, Medicare is a federal program under which coverage decisions are made by companies in each state that process claims for Medicare. It essentially works like a Preferred Provider Organization (PPO). It is flexible in terms of giving you your choice of providers. Medicare Advantage (Part C) programs act more as HMOs, which have strict limits on your choices of providers. You will be required to use providers and facilities within the plan's network. In addition to this limitation, there can be hidden and unexpected costs that you would not have with traditional Medicare. This usually applies to sicker people. For most of my career, I have consulted with clients who are already using a myriad of long term care services. I have noticed that for those who have Medicare Advantage plans, the sicker and more reliant on the medical system they become, the less their plan works well for them. Since Medicare Advantage plans must accept any Medicare-eligible participant, they off-set that risk by having more stringent coverage rules and denials happen more frequently than with Original Medicare. Generally, once one reaches a certain point, leaving their Medicare Advantage plan to enroll in traditional Medicare with a supplement makes more sense financially, no matter how low the Medicare Advantage premium is. Of course, this is not a blanket statement, it is simply a generalized observation. I am not saying Medicare Advantage plans are all bad and should be avoided. As with everything else, my primary encouragement to you is to be an educated consumer and compare your options diligently before making a decision.

By the time you find yourself in a caregiving role, it is entirely possible that your care recipient has already enrolled in Medicare. They will automatically be enrolled in Original Medicare when they become eligible for social security or when they qualify for disability and receive SSDI for two years. If they are over 65 and not yet receiving Social Security, then they will have to enroll in both Medicare Part A and B. It is important to know what the Medicare co-pays, deductibles and coinsurance amounts are to budget appropriately for out-of-pocket medical costs each year. Annually you will have the opportunity to revisit plan options and make enrollment decisions. Your care recipient may need to purchase a Medicare Supplement (sometimes referred to as "Medigap plans") which are offered by private insurance companies to help cover deductibles and copays. Medicaid, which we will discuss later, can also serve as a secondary payor to Medicare.

Your care recipient will be able to make Medicare enrollment decisions during their personal initial enrollment period, (IEP) which is three months before, the month of, and the three months following the month during which they turn age 65.[41] Failing to enroll during this period can trigger penalties and coverage gaps. If your care recipient misses their IEP, they need to be aware of the other annual enrollment windows. Medicare's General Enrollment Period (for traditional Medicare or Medicare Advantage plans) runs Jan. 1 to March 31. If your care recipient enrolls during this time, their coverage will be effective July 1. Current enrollees can make changes to their plans or coverage options during the Open Enrollment Period which runs from Oct. 15 through Dec. 7, with coverage becoming effective Jan. 1 of the following year.[42]

Medicare beneficiaries can enroll in or drop Medicare Supplement plans at any time. You can also disenroll from a Medicare Advantage plan and opt back into Original Medicare (and even enroll in a Medicare Supplement plan) during the first 12 months of the date that you enrolled in the Medicare Advantage plan. After this initial 12 month period, you can change policies or enroll back into Original

---

[41] medicare.gov
[42] medicare.gov/basics/get-started-with-medicare

Medicare during the annual Open Enrollment period.

Penalties and increased premiums can be imposed due to failure to enroll during the appropriate enrollment period. For Part A, you may be assessed a 10 percent increase in monthly premium if you do not qualify for premium-free coverage and fail to enroll on time. This penalty is imposed for double the number of years that you delayed enrolling. So, two years for every one year you delayed enrolling. For Part B, if you do not enroll when you first become eligible, you may also be assessed a 10 percent penalty for each 12-month period you would have been eligible for Part B. The worst part is that this penalty lasts for as long as you are enrolled in Medicare. The penalty amount for Part D is 1 percent of the "National Base Premium" for the total number of months that you delay enrolling. Like Part B, the Part D penalties are imposed for as long as you are enrolled in Medicare. Most importantly, remember that enrollment in Part D is never automatic. You cannot be passive about this process and expect to avoid penalties.[43]

HOW DO YOU GET HELP WITH MEDICARE?

Medicare enrollment can be a daunting task. As we have already covered, there are a multitude of plans, coverage options, and enrollment rules. Even if your care recipient already has their Medicare plan(s) in place, it is still important for you to understand how Medicare works. You should also routinely evaluate what plan(s) they are enrolled in to determine if it is the best coverage for their situation. If it isn't, you need to be aware of the opportunities to make changes each year to ensure you do not miss important cut off dates.

You can find resources and enroll online,[44] however, my suggestion would be to sit down with a professional advisor on a regular basis to review your care recipient's coverage and consider what plan(s) make the most sense for your individual medical and financial situation. A qualified insurance professional is a good resource to have on your advocacy team. In most places, the Area Agency on Aging can help you with this.

---

[43] medicare.gov/basics/get-started-with-medicare
[44] medicare.gov/basics/get-started-with-medicare or benefitscheckup.org

Medicaid is also federal money that is managed at a state level. It has two parts, the first is health insurance for eligible low-income adults, children, pregnant women, elderly adults and people with disabilities. The second part is for long term care.

There are strict income and asset limits related to qualifying for Medicaid. At the average monthly Social Security benefit of $1,5470 per month,[45] the average senior cannot afford to pay out of pocket for long-term care. Medicaid for long term care is designed to support those people. That being said, it should be considered a final fail safe. If your care recipient does have assets available to use for their long-term care, this is a blessing. Using your own resources gives you many more options and allows you to remain in control of your finances. It is my personal opinion that those who have it should use it to pay for their own care, and Medicaid should be reserved for those who truly need it.

Applications for Medicaid are processed through the Department of Social Services. There are different Medicaid programs depending on the locale that can help pay for long-term care.

Coverage varies from state to state, but Medicaid will generally cover:

- Long-term care in a nursing facility

- Assisted Living Auxiliary grant (extremely limited)

- In-home health care services

Keep in mind that while coverage for home care services may exist, currently the programs tend to largely be more favorable towards institutional care versus care in the home. Therefore, it can be difficult to secure quality, consistent Medicaid-funded care in the home setting. While community Medicaid and Nursing Home Medicaid are different, qualifying for the community program first and transitioning to the nursing home program is much easier than starting from scratch upon nursing home admission.

---

[45] ssa.gov/policy/docs/quickfacts/stat_snapshot/

Furthermore, while the nursing homes do usually have staff such as social workers that assist with applying for Medicaid for residents who may need it, they are generally not experts in the subject and are just doing the bare minimum necessary to submit the application. This means they will not be very helpful in actually seeing the process to fruition, and will leave most of the heavy lifting up to the family. Also, while most are well intentioned, they are not qualified to give legal advice. The exception to this is when the resident has no assets of any value in their name and the qualification will be very straightforward.

If your care recipient has minimal assets and intends to rely on Medicaid for their long term care funding, do not fall victim to the common assumption that advance planning is pointless. Planning ahead can help avoid the stressors of securing long term care due to the processing times and waiting lists involved. Way too often, Medicaid eligible care recipients do not apply for Medicaid until they are placed in a nursing home. It is my advice to not wait until that happens to start the process. Getting qualified in advance of the need will allow for ample time to handle it correctly and it will also give you more flexibility in choosing a preferred facility.

If there are financial assets available, the overarching goal should be to identify ways to make them last as long as possible and take care of those who are living. Too often, the approach taken is to hide as much money as possible for the benefit of their heirs after they have passed and get on Medicaid as soon as possible during their lifetime. When people do this, they do not necessarily realize the implications of using Medicaid to pay for care instead of their own funds. Or perhaps, they are being taken advantage of by greedy heirs.

There are times that it is prudent to identify ways to save some or all of their assets for later use for themselves or someone in their family that may need it (such as a spouse or special needs child). Sometimes people are interested in preserving specific assets for legacy purposes (such as property or business assets that have been passed down in the family). Other times it is apparent that the individual will need nursing home care and does not have sufficient resources to pay for it, so Medicaid planning may be necessary to avoid missteps in the Medicaid Qualification process. There may even be a need to undo things that have already been done incorrectly. Furthermore, spending down all of what they do have now may prevent them from being able to use any of it in the future when their care needs are greater. If you find yourself in any of these predicaments, or any other justifiable reason for preserving assets, it is advisable to consult with a qualified attorney that is familiar with this very complicated area of the law for guidance. Many legal firms offer a service called Medicaid Planning. Medicaid planning is a process designed to protect all or a portion of an individual's assets while setting them up to qualify for Medicaid. This kind of strategic planning is complex and must be done well in advance of needing long-term care services, as the lookback period for Medicaid applications in most states is five years. This means that during the five year period prior to applying for Medicaid, transfers of assets and certain financial transactions could be considered gifts and trigger a penalty. During the penalty period the applicant would not be eligible for Medicaid which can truly be problematic when there are no assets to use for care. These transactions could be anything from cash gifts to property deed transfers to giving a vehicle to a family member. Anything sold without proper documentation and at fair market value can cause problems.

One concern that is common for older adults is whether the nursing home will take their home. When one moves into a nursing home and will be using Medicaid to pay, they will have to spend down their assets first. These assets can include cash, retirement and investment accounts, stocks, bonds, and real property. Some assets are considered exempt such as a vehicle and the applicant's primary home as long as they or their spouse are living in it. Furthermore, assets that were transferred into irrevocable Medicaid-compliant trusts prior to the lookback period will be exempt.

The bottom line is that the nursing facility does not "take" the applicant's home. However, the state may force the applicant to sell the home and use the proceeds to pay for their care before Medicaid will kick in. The applicant must show good faith effort to sell the home while Medicaid is pending (unless a

---

[46] naela.org

spouse is living in it, or some other rare exception applies).

An elder law attorney can help you understand the Medicaid qualification process fully, and outline for you the potential options for protecting and preserving assets. Your advocacy team should consist of an experienced elder law attorney that you can speak to about such matters. If you do not already have one in place, you can locate one either by referral or through the national association website.[46] There is also a guide included with this chapter that will help you prepare for the process of medicaid planning.

FAMILY CARE WAIVERS

In some cases, Medicaid may provide payment directly to a caregiver providing care to an elderly or disabled family member living in the community. This is known as a "Self-directed" or Consumer-directed" waiver. In most states, adult children and other family members can be paid by Medicaid for providing personal care for their family members, but spouses cannot. Generally, the family member will be required to undergo some level of formal training and meet certain requirements first, and the client must still be screened and determined to meet eligibility requirements both financially and physically. The rate of pay is usually less than desirable, but for many, it is better to receive even minimum wage than to work entirely uncompensated if working otherwise is made impossible by the need for family care.

To receive payment from Medicaid for caring for your care recipient, you must go through the same application and qualification process as you would for Agency-directed care, just through a different department. This program is called community-based care or self-directed care. This hired family member is treated just like an employee and must submit regular timesheets and documentation to Medicaid to be eligible for ongoing payment. Sometimes the state will require the family caregiver be hired by a third-party agency and submit the documentation through the agency. Should your Medicaid program allow you to hire the caregiver directly and not go through an agency, be sure to follow the guidance provided in chapter three regarding privately hiring a caregiver. The same advice applies even if the caregiver is family.

Now, let's circle back to the U! The process of determining how your care recipient will pay for care is multifaceted. The first step will be sitting down with your care recipient (if they are of sound mind- if not, this task is considerably more challenging) and gathering all the facts and data about their finances. This part of your planning may be particularly challenging because many older adults are hesitant to share information about their finances, even with their family. But, when you are making decisions about care for them, finances are a tremendously necessary consideration. The discussion may not be comfortable, but it is necessary. Again, have this conversation when your care recipient is of sound mind and body. Doing so will make things much easier for you when you do need to step in.

What do you need to know? Consider asking the following questions to start:

- Is there a long-term care or other type of insurance policy that can be used?
- What other resources are available to pay for long term care?
- What money is coming in? (Retirement funds, Pension, etc.)
- What money is going out? (Bills, rent or mortgage, insurance, etc.)

INSURANCE

Long Term Care Insurance If your care recipient has long-term care insurance, consider yourself lucky! This is what you should use first to fund their long-term care. Many plans will cover both in-home care services and assisted living, but one option may be covered more favorably than another. The first step is to find the benefits summary or call the insurance company to find out what benefits they have. You will also need to ask what the requirements are to qualify for them.

If your care recipient does not have a long-term care insurance policy, securing it now will be extremely difficult, most likely impossible. They require a medical screening, and costs increase significantly for people of advanced age. It can be a challenge to determine what the sweet spot is for securing this type of insurance, but in general your early to mid-fifties tend to be a good time to purchase a policy if you are generally healthy.

In most cases the policyholder using the services must pay for the services first, then are reimbursed by the policy after submitting paid invoices and other required documentation. Understanding up front what is required to get your claims paid and staying on top of it will serve you well. See the guide I put together on long term care insurance claims for this chapter for guidance submitting the claims. Also, be sure to talk to your provider (facility or home care) before admission to determine if they will process the long-term care invoices for you or if you are on your own to do it. Be forewarned, this is a lot of work. It is well worth the effort to search for a provider that will do it for you or assist you in doing it.

Finally, be advised that your care recipient's care needs may not be covered completely by their policy. Policies will have a maximum daily, monthly, and/ or lifetime benefit. It is important to find out upfront what those limits are so that you can plan your budget for long-term care services accordingly. If a couple is relying on long term care insurance to fund their care, it is important to understand the limitations on using the policy by each of the spouses. Do they have a shared care plan? Meaning, when one spouse's benefit is used up can they draw on the other's to pay for their care? This flexibility can be very beneficial when one spouse is diagnosed with a chronic illness and the other remains healthy. However, consider how the other will pay for their care if both spouse's benefits are used up caring for one. I had a couple that we cared for in our home care company that had a shared care benefit. It was a blessing to them when the husband was diagnosed with Parkinson's disease. He used up his entire two year benefit maximum and dipped into hers for his third year using our services. He continued using the benefit until it ran out, leaving the caregiving spouse with nothing for her own care in the future. It didn't take long before she needed it, after an unsuccessful hip surgery kept her from getting fully back on her feet again shortly after his passing. She ended up using Medicaid services for her care which were less reliable and often frustrating for her. My company did not take Medicaid, so I had to refer her out to another local company that did. I continued to visit and she would call me on and off on a regular basis to complain about the service of the Medicaid company.

In hindsight, it may have made more sense for her to place her husband on Medicaid care while he was still living and save some of her benefit for herself.

Life Insurance. Some life insurance policies can also help offset long-term care expenses. Some policies have a provision that is called an "accelerated death benefit," meaning you can withdraw tax-free cash advances to use while you are living. Policy provisions around this benefit will vary, but some will allow this benefit to be used when you are using qualified long-term care services. There may be other qualifiers. Usually, the benefit is limited to up to 70 or 80 percent of the policy value.

Your care recipient may also be able to sell their life insurance policy to use it for long term care. This provision is called a "life settlement," and is sometimes an option for people who are over age 70. This cash advance is not tax-free, but there are generally no restrictions on what you can use the money for, unlike the accelerated death benefit. Some plans will also offer a "viatical settlement," which allows a terminally ill person to sell their policy for a percentage of the death benefit.

Of course, doing any of these things means the policy-holder's beneficiaries will get less, but usually by this stage in life adult children are financially secure enough on their own that this is less of a concern for older adults.

Annuities. Annuities are also an insurance product designed to help supplement your income in retirement and pay for potential long-term care services. They do not have the same medical underwriting requirements as long term care and life insurance. Essentially, you are purchasing a guaranteed income stream, guarding against the risk of outliving your resources. There are several different types of annuities. The favorable tax treatment by the IRS is one reason annuities can be an attractive option. However, you must have the up front cash to put down to purchase the annuity. To determine if an annuity would be right for your care recipient, seek advice from a qualified financial advisor.

OTHER FUNDING SOURCES

In the absence of insurance coverage, your care recipient's private funds will need to be used to pay for any long-term care needs that crop up that are not covered by Medicare. Before turning to Medicaid, your care recipient's personal savings and retirement funds will need to be exhausted to pay for long-term care. Be sure to investigate all possible sources available. Your care recipient may have stashed away savings in a place they do not even remember. Do a thorough search, leave no stone unturned. One of the biggest hurdles to overcome is that many older adults have assets scattered across multiple banks and investment firms. If this is the case, investigate ways to simplify things for yourself. Consolidating as much as possible may be a good first step. It is also very common for older adults to be hesitant to spend their money. They may have pinched and saved their entire lives and then in their retirement they live from social security check to social security check, hesitant to spend any of their hard-earned funds. I would frequently hear "we cannot afford that" from an older adult who was by all appearances struggling to get by when in fact, they had plenty of money in their savings account for the services they desperately needed.

My clients, Mr. and Mrs. Phillips are a prime example. When I met them, Mr. Phillips was in his upper 80s while Mrs. Phillips was 92. Mrs. Phillips had Alzheimer's disease and an array of health challenges. She was wheelchair bound, and Mr. Phillips had to provide nearly all of her personal care. He had been doing this for seven years at the time his daughter Angela called me in. Angela was worried about her father killing himself to take care of her mother. His self-care was faltering and he had been hospitalized twice in the past several months when she called. He was wearing himself out. They lived in a 100-year-old farmhouse that was severely in need of repair. Their bedroom was up a flight of stairs that I didn't even feel safe walking up. I truly cannot even imagine how he got her up and down those stairs every day.

During an initial assessment, one of my questions is always about the available resources for care and services. When I asked Mr. Phillips what funding sources were available for care, he quickly told me that they had no way to pay for care and they would need Medicaid, but he was afraid he would lose the house so he had not applied for it. He asked if I could help him with this. Angela spoke up, saying "Dad, what about your retirement account at Merrill Lynch?". He flinched and replied "That is our rainy-day fund Angela. We can't use that money." I paused, and then I asked, "Mr. Phillips, how much money is in your rainy-day fund?". He said "Oh, about $190,000.00 I believe. But that is for emergencies only." I glanced at Angela and she gave me an exasperated look. I turned back to Mr. Phillips, looked him square in the face and I said, "Mr. Phillips, it is pouring. It is time to use that money." He was taken aback. He didn't say anything at first. Then, he slowly turned to Angela and told her to call their financial advisor and set up a meeting.

I tell you this story to encourage you to emphasize to your care recipient that the reason they saved their money is to use it for themselves when they needed it– which is now! Don't let them struggle and worry when they have savings they can tap into. Tomorrow is not guaranteed, use the money now to make life easier during a difficult time.

In addition to their own savings, there are some other funding sources that can be used to pay for long term care, which are worth looking into:

Veterans Administration. If your care recipient or their spouse spent time in the military they may qualify for financial support or other benefits from the Veterans Administration. However, some of the programs the Veterans Administration offers seem like the best-kept secrets in long-term care. Navigating the VA and its programs can be quite strenuous. Contact a local VA benefits office for assistance, and have your veteran's discharge papers handy when you do.

Trusts. We touched on trusts when we covered legal planning in an earlier chapter. A trust is a legal entity that an individual can set up and transfer a portion of their assets into, sometimes to help pay for long term care services later. A Trust is a good way to ensure assets are protected for an older adult or someone with special needs, but the key to ensuring that protection is control of the Trust by someone else. This means the principal has no say over how the assets in the Trust are used. This type of Trust also must be irrevocable (meaning it cannot be revoked or changed later). This relinquishing of control is often unnerving for older adults. Of course, there are many different types of Trusts. It is prudent to speak with an attorney that specializes in this area to determine if a Trust is right for your care recipient and what type of Trust will work best for their individual situation.

Home Equity. For many older adults, their home is their largest asset and perhaps their only asset. The equity in the home may be tapped into through a line of credit to pay for in-home care. A reverse mortgage is a common term for the Federal Home Equity Conversion Mortgage (HECM) program. With this program, the equity in the home may be tapped into through a line of credit to pay for in-home care, home remodifications, or other living expenses. This type of loan is repaid when the owner sells the home or passes away. If you do not anticipate that your care recipient will be able to remain at home long term, a reverse mortgage may not be the best option for them as once the equity is withdrawn and spent on current care expenses, it will no longer be available later to downsize, move into an assisted living facility, or to pay for care while living with a family member. There is a lot of confusion around how these work, be sure to educate yourself thoroughly. The federal trade commission website is a good place to start.[47]

Another option for a homeowner is selling the home and using the profit for assisted living or nursing home care. An older adult considering selling their home may want to consult with a certified Seniors Real Estate Specialist, who is trained in the unique needs and challenges of buying and selling for seniors. Many SRES Realtors will also assist their clients in locating a multitude of different resources to assist them with their complex needs.

Community Based Resources. Many community-based services such as meal delivery, wellness visits and adult day care are offered either for free or reduced prices by local government agencies or nonprofit organizations.

Grants. Grants are not plentiful nor easy to obtain. There are only two that I am familiar with, and they are caregiving grants for people living with Alzheimer's disease or other dementias. The first is through the Alzheimer's Foundation,[48] and the second is through Hilarity for Charity.[49] It is not my intention to offer false hope, so to be clear, these grants are hard to win. Furthermore, they will generally cover only a minimal amount of respite hours per year. Nevertheless, they are worth mentioning as any little bit helps!

---

[47] consumer.ftc.gov/articles/reverse-mortgages
[48] alzfdn.org/find-a-member/grant-information/
[49] helpforalzheimersfamilies.com/Hilarity-for-Charity/

Once you have your arms around what the available resources are, the next step is to work closely with your care recipient's advocacy team to come up with a sustainable plan for their care. As you and your advocacy team create this comprehensive plan it should include how and where they want to live, what type of care they may need, and what resources are available. But one of the key questions is– how much will you need to plan for? Estimating how much money is needed is a tricky part of the planning. I will remind you of the GUESS acronym, and point out the "U" for understanding yet again. You must first seek to understand the needs and risks. Based on personal experiences and family health history, you can get a good idea of what your care recipient's elder years may look like. It is very important to consider the potential for chronic illnesses that run in their family, such as Alzheimer's disease, when making your plan. You will want to ensure that you plan for the likelihood of increasing care needs and inflation of long-term care costs over time. Consider worst-case scenarios and plan accordingly by developing a strategy to offset the risks.

Once you and your advocacy team have conducted an analysis of current and future care needs, research must be done into what types of services are available in the community where your care recipient lives and the associated costs. Pricing is all over the map when it comes to both home care and senior community living. Furthermore, availability and access to services varies greatly depending on geography and other factors. Do your best to take a wide sampling of types and costs of services so that you do not underestimate. Then, the next step is to make a budget for how long they can afford each type of service and the likelihood that they may outlive their resources. It can be tempting to choose the senior living solution that is the best your care recipient can afford in their current financial situation. However, If resources are limited, choosing a long term care service that can also be funded by a public payor source such as Medicaid may be the best option to avoid service interruptions.

A qualified financial advisor is a valuable resource as a part of the advocacy team. This type of professional can give advice on what money to use first, in what order, to minimize taxes and maximize the longevity of resources.

One common mistake is putting all your eggs in one basket when it comes to investments. This can be risky and may not have a good long-term outcome. Your care recipient's current portfolio may not be ideal for the stage of life they are facing next. The financial advisor can aid you in identifying where the losses are and ways to optimize finances. If your care recipient does not have a relationship with a financial advisor, it may be prudent to find one now. They will comb through and look at everything and help you get organized, set up a plan, and update it regularly as your care recipient's needs change.

Is your caregiving experience pressing you to start thinking about your own long-term care planning? A combination of long term care insurance, self-funding, and a solid caregiving plan is what I would strongly recommend. First understand your potential needs and risks, and then determine how much of that risk you are willing and able to bear yourself and what you want or need to pass on. Then, I reiterate the importance of consulting with professionals who can guide you and help you project your anticipated care costs, so that you can sleep soundly at night knowing you are well prepared.

THE CAREGIVER'S FINANCIAL BURDEN

You need to be aware of your own financial exposure as a caregiver. I have spoken to many caregivers who are forced to dip into their own savings or cut back on their household budget for things such as eating out, extracurricular activities or vacations. This can put added strain on your family and contribute to tension between you and your care recipient. While my primary piece of advice is to avoid getting into this situation with good advance planning, sometimes that is easier said than done. The following tips may help you if you find yourself in unavoidable financial strain as a caregiver.

If you are the sole or primary caregiver, consider asking your family to pitch in to pay you for your services. I recognize this is a sensitive subject for many. Not only is talk of money uncomfortable, but it can be very difficult to determine what the true value of caregiving is. Also, other family members who are not the primary may also pitch in to help from time to time- so they may expect commensurate enumeration.

There are conditions under which you may be able to be paid by your care recipient's insurance, the Veterans Administration, or as mentioned earlier through a consumer directed program under Medicaid. Consulting an elder law attorney about these options is the best approach to avoid any pitfalls and ensure things are done properly.

There are also many expenses related to caregiving that you can deduct on your tax return so be sure to keep good documentation of any out-of-pocket expenditures. Things like mileage to and from appointments, supplies like briefs and wipes, personal protective equipment, even meals and lodging if you are staying in a hotel while your care recipient receives medical care, for example. Additionally, if your care recipient lives with you and you pay for a minimum of 50 percent of their expenses, you may be able to claim them as a dependent.[50] Seek out a certified public accountant that is well versed in this area of the tax laws to add to your advocacy team. Keep good records and save receipts for all expenses. If you aren't sure whether something will count or not, keep track of it anyway; the professionals can help you sort it out later.

You may also be wondering if you can be held financially responsible for your care recipient's bills. It is true that about 30 states* have filial responsibility laws that put the burden of responsibility for long-term care costs of indigent seniors on their adult children.[51] It is uncommon, however, for these laws to be enforced. Your primary responsibility as an agent is to ensure that your care recipient's funds are used appropriately. Nevertheless, when signing any legal contract on your care recipient's behalf, read the document carefully. When in doubt, consult an attorney before signing anything. You may be advised to sign as the agent and not as the responsible party. This does not mean you are required to foot the bill when they run out of money. However, you are likely to be held responsible for applying for Medicaid timely and honestly.

*States with filial responsibility laws: Alaska, Arkansas, California, Connecticut, Delaware, Georgia, Idaho, Indiana, Iowa, Kentucky, Louisiana, Maryland, Massachusetts, Mississippi, Montana, Nevada, New Hampshire, New Jersey, North Carolina, North Dakota, Ohio, Oregon, Pennsylvania, Rhode Island, South Dakota, Tennessee, Utah, Vermont, Virginia, and West Virginia

---

[50] irs.gov/faqs/irs-procedures/for-caregivers
[51] Filial Responsibility: Can the Legal Duty to Support Our Parents Be Effectively Enforced? by Shannon Frank Edelstone, appearing in the Fall 2002 issue of the American Bar Association's Family Law Quarterly, 36 Fam. L.Q. 501 (2002). Lexic.com

MEDICARE COVERAGE AND NON COVERAGE LIST

In general, you can expect Original Medicare to cover*:

- Inpatient hospital stays (when you have met the admission criteria)
- Skilled nursing facility care (when you have met the admission criteria)
- Hospice care
- Home health care
- Medically necessary ambulance transportation
- Durable Medical Equipment
- Outpatient therapy
- Doctor's visits
- Preventative vaccines such as flu shots
- Preventative health screenings
- Medically necessary labs, x-rays and tests
- Medically necessary surgeries (not optional or cosmetic surgeries)

In general, you can expect Original Medicare to not cover:

- Long term care in a nursing facility or other senior living community (custodial)
- Most dental and vision care (including dentures)
- Routine podiatry care
- Hearing aids
- Prescription drugs (unless you are enrolled in Part D)

You are responsible for deductibles and copayments

MEDICAID PLANNING PREPARATION

This checklist will help you when preparing for a Medicaid planning consultation with an elder law attorney.*

- Copies of Medicare and any other insurance cards
- Identification/proof of citizenship
- Proof of all sources of income (check stubs, direct deposit summary)
- Proof of residence.
- Recent property tax bills (including their primary home and any other property they own or partially own)
- Bank statements for all financial accounts (at least 12 months). This includes investments, stocks. Bonds, etc.
- Most recent income tax return
- Registration for any vehicles in their name
- All insurance policy information
- A list of all recurring expenses. For example: mortgage or rent, utilities, car insurance, health insurance premiums, etc.
- Face and cash values of all life and long term care insurance policies
- Documentation related to any prepaid burial or funeral plans
- Copy of Will/Trust
- All marriage and divorce certificates for any legal marriage

Every state has different Medicaid eligibility rules. This guide is meant to provide basic organizational advice to help you be prepared and the process go smoothly.

LONG TERM CARE INSURANCE CLAIMS

This guide outlines the process to submit a long term care insurance claim.

Step 1: Opening the Claim

- The policyholder (or their agent) must contact the insurance carrier to open the claim (the telephone number of the carrier is typically listed on the first page of the policy)
- Note: If the caller is not the policyholder, the policyholder will be required to give permission to speak to the caller
  - If the agent is to be the ongoing point of contact, the carrier will likely require a copy of their Power of Attorney
- Have the following ready for the call:
  - The policy number
  - The policyholder's current address
  - The first four consecutive digits of the policyholder's social security number
- The carrier will request documentation from the facility or home care provider to determine that they are an eligible provider
  - This may include their state license and/or business license, insurance policies or other documentation

Step 2: Eligibility determination

- The carrier will sometimes require the policyholder to undergo a screening by a licensed Health Care Practitioner (HCP)*
  - Typically, it will be necessary for claimant to require assistance with 2 out of 6 Activities of Daily Living (day to day activities, such as bathing, dressing, toileting and ambulation), or to be considered to have a serious cognitive impairment such as Alzhiemer's disease
  - The carrier may request additional medical records or information from the policyholder's physician to provide support for the claim
- The carrier determines if the policyholder's care provider meets the policy requirements and notifies the policyholder in writing

Step 3: Elimination period
- Almost all policies have an elimination period, which is a waiting period before benefits are paid; it is usually between 60-120 days in duration
- During this time, the policyholder must pay for service while remaining eligible for benefits, similar to a deductible

Step 4: Submitting invoices
- The policyholder must submit written invoices for covered services in to receive policy benefits
- The carrier may also request copies of the care plan and care related documentation
- Most policies will reimburse the policyholder for qualifying expenses (in some cases, the policyholder may choose to have the carrier pay the service provider directly– this is called an Assignment of Benefits)

Step 5: Ongoing Eligibility Determinations
- The carrier will review the Long Term Care Insurance claim periodically to ensure the policyholder remains eligible for benefits
- The carrier may on occasion request an updated care plan from the provider of services

I recommend having an advocate (a family member or caregiver) present with the care recipient during the assessment by a Health Care Provider. Older adults tend to answer questions hesitantly and don't like to admit shortcomings, so having someone there that can give an accurate picture of their needs is very helpful to avoid unfair denials. For example, your loved one may say "yes I can bathe myself." But you know that how they do so is very unsafe, and having a skilled caregiver present would make bathing much safer and easier for your loved one. Therefore, you can interject with "while my loved one does bathe herself, it is a struggle, and having supervision to do so would be a much safer option."

NOTES

NOTES

CHAPTER 6

CARING FOR THE CAREGIVER

*The best way to find yourself is to lose yourself
in service of others.* -Ghandi

We have reviewed a lot of information thus far. You may be overwhelmed. If so, pause and take a deep breath. You now know how to advocate for your care recipient, what some of the different care options are, and you may realize that planning ahead for the potential needs of your care recipient is the right thing to do. Hopefully, you feel better equipped to get started on your caregiving journey.

Last but certainly not least, let's talk about you. Yes, you! I realize that when you are wrapped up in the all-consuming world of caregiving, it feels like everything is always about your care recipient. This entire book up to this point has been about how to take the best care of someone else. But, let's put the spotlight on you for a moment.

The act of caregiving requires an immense amount of multitasking, prioritizing, and sacrificing. It is a balancing act that quite simply cannot always be perfectly managed, and stress is an inevitable consequence. Many caregivers, especially those of the Sandwich Generation, experience high levels of stress related to the fact that there is simply not enough time in the day to get everything done, and they constantly feel like they are forgetting or neglecting responsibilities. That stress is dangerous and can lead to a number of ailments. Many caregivers are sick and struggling day in and day out. This level of stress can even take years off a caregiver's life. One of the most staggering statistics I have read related to this phenomenon was in a study conducted by psychiatrists at the University of Pittsburgh, which reported that the caregivers in the study who were providing care and experiencing caregiver strain had mortality risks that were 63 percent higher than non-caregiving controls.[52] Those caring for a care recipient living with dementia have been shown to experience an even greater negative impact on their immune system for up to three years after their caregiving experience is over, thus increasing their chances of developing a chronic illness themselves.[53]

Learning to manage stress is of utmost importance for caregivers, and will help avoid a serious condition known as Caregiver Burnout. Caregiver Burnout is the phenomenon in which physical and mental exhaustion consume you, making it difficult to function normally. Burnout is common for those who have taken on a caregiving role, whether expected or unexpected. While similar to depression in terms of symptoms, Caregiver Burnout is more than depression alone. While it is normal to experience a myriad of negative emotions, and to feel overwhelmed, Caregiver Burnout goes beyond that. This condition builds up over a long period of time under stress and pressure, and it can be completely debilitating. It is severely threatening to physical and mental health, potentially leading to premature aging and illness.

Many caregivers are spouses, some the same age or even older than their partner they are caring for. And given that the average life expectancy continues

---

[52] Caregiving as a Risk Factor for Mortality The Caregiver Health Effects Study, Journal of the American Medical Association, DECEMBER 15, 1999 Richard Schulz, PhD; Scott R. Beach, PhD
[53] National Alliance for Caregiving and AARP. (2009). Caregiving in the U.S

climbing, we find many adult children in their 60s and 70s caring for aging parents in their 80s and 90s. Elderly caregivers are often dealing with their own health issues and overall physical decline that comes with aging. Combine this with Caregiver Burnout and it can be extremely dangerous to have "the blind leading the blind."

I once had a client, Norma, who engaged my company when she needed help caring for her husband, Gerald. Gerald had Parkinson's and suffered from dementia associated with the illness. He was a retired Navy Captain. When I met Gerald he was able to communicate intelligibly. He mostly struggled with mobility. He would get up in the morning and Norma would help him get out of bed and use a walker to go into the living room where he sat in a chair that lifted to assist with standing up. He stayed in that chair most of the day only getting up to use the bathroom. He would even eat his meals in the chair. She was an avid bridge and mahjong player. One of her favorite pastimes was playing with the other residents of the independent senior living community where she and Gerald lived. Gerald was content to sit and read while she went down to the common areas for social gatherings and meals on her own.

Over the course of two years his decline was tremendous. He was a tall man (over 6 ft.) and while he was thin, it was very difficult for Norma, who was not a tall woman, to transfer him from bed to chair or chair to wheelchair. There were several times that Gerald fell and almost hurt Norma severely. This was a dangerous scenario. However, in spite of the challenges, she was determined to care for him on her own (with some help from our agency but she would only use as much as her long term care insurance would cover, so she received about 6 hours of caregiving services 6 days per week).

Norma's self care faltered drastically while she was caring for her husband. She had a bad back, hips and knees and she was putting off any surgery for herself due to caring for Gerald. She stopped participating in her card games because she couldn't leave him alone. She had even stopped going to church services. Once our caregiver got wind of this she asked if she could volunteer for the two hours on Sunday mornings to allow Norma to go to church while she stayed with Gerald, so at least she was able to continue going to church.

Furthermore, she had diabetes and struggled to prepare healthy food for herself that met her dietary requirements. She gained weight, and became depressed. Her eyesight worsened and it became hard for her to read or knit like she loved doing. I saw first hand what caregiver burnout was doing to her. Despite our consistent urging, she always put Gerald first and her health took a drastic turn for the worse. There was more than one occasion that I was visiting Norma and Gerald in their home and would hear Norma on the phone with either their son or their daughter. Each time, I would hear her tell them that she was doing just fine. The children were not local and did not visit often. Norma hid her caregiving struggles from her children because she did not want to burden them. After he passed, it was only a little over a year before she passed away herself. I admired Norma for her dedication to her spouse, but I wish she would not have lost sight of herself in the process.

I reiterate, Caregiver Burnout is a real risk to physical and mental health. You may already be experiencing it, or perhaps you can feel it coming. Remember, you cannot take care of your care recipient if you do not take care of yourself. It is like the airplane instruction to secure your own oxygen mask before securing someone else's; you can't take care of others without first taking care of yourself. Caregivers must prioritize their own health and strike a balance of caregiving with self-care.

So how does one avoid Caregiver burnout? Believe me, I know it sounds much easier said than done! However, I am pleased to inform you that in relation to the first strategy for this you are already well on your way just by reading this book. That is hatching a plan. The primary solution to avoiding a painful case of caregiver burnout is good planning, because in doing so you will spend less time correcting the course of the ship when it goes off track. You will save yourself a lot of stress by having a good plan and support team in place.

Next, we should address sharing the caregiving burden. When you bear the burden of caregiving alone, it is almost inevitable that you will experience burnout and neglect other areas of your life at some point. Therefore, if you have multiple family members who must come together to determine how to care for your care recipient, first things first- count your blessings. There are many people out there who are the only child or do not have siblings who are able or willing to help. However, those with family still might feel alone! If you find that you are bearing the brunt of the caregiving responsibilities in your family and are feeling overwhelmed, remember two of my top five tips —set boundaries and seek support! Sometimes all it takes is speaking up to bring to others attention that you need their help. I find oftentimes there are natural leaders in the family that will naturally take on most of the work, not ask for help, and then end up feeling resentful that they did not get the help they needed. Consider that they really may not be aware that you are struggling, they may think you have it all together or they may think you don't want them to intrude.

Before jumping headfirst into this pivotal conversation, take time to consider what type of help you really want and then talk to them. In doing so, be aware of the factors that can influence if and how family members can help. It is important to not have unrealistic expectations. For example, quite often geography plays a large factor. Whomever lives closest to the care recipient is the one able to most regularly check in on them and assist when needed. Other factors might be employment status, the relationship with the care recipient, and even financial stability. Many families will come up with a way to divide the responsibility that takes these factors into account. For example, the one who lives the closest may handle the shopping and doctor's appointments, while the one that lives further away may use online banking to pay bills and manage the finances, or even use the internet to do research on resources in the care recipient's hometown.

You may find yourself in the opposite situation. Perhaps your sibling or other family member is taking the lead in caring for your care recipient and you want to help but do not know how. Keep in mind that simply asking the primary caregiver in your family how you can help may not be the best way to get involved. It can be difficult for a caregiver to take a step back and identify where they need help or what you can do to alleviate some of the burden. A better approach may be to just jump in and do it. But in doing so be sure the communication is clear so there is not overlapping efforts or undue confusion. Poor communication is most frequently at the root of some of the biggest family issues. Try something like "I am free on thursday and could take mom to her doctor's appointment, would that be helpful for you?". This gives the primary caregiver the opportunity to accept your help without "stepping on toes".

At times it can be hard for families to all come to a consensus on how to handle the care needs, the finances, the household, and other things. When I first started out working as a social worker in a nursing home, I was introduced to this concept as "family dynamics". When a family was constantly disagreeing or quarreling over care decisions, it was the polite term we used for it in our notes. "Mrs. Smith's family expressed multiple issues related to *family dynamics* in the care plan meeting" decoded means: "Mrs. Smith's family fights a lot". Disagreements can lead to arguments, hurt feelings and even broken relationships. The goal should always be to avoid this, but it is hard not to let our emotions get in the way when discussing care decisions.

If you find yourself in the midst of "family dynamics", the best way to handle it is to bring in a professional. An unbiased advocate who can help mediate. As I have mentioned, an Aging Life Care manager can function in this role- becoming the "coach" or "team captain" for the family as a whole, and assisting them in making sound decisions for their care recipient's care. You could also seek the guidance of a family counselor or licensed clinical social worker. The primary function of bringing a professional in should not be to support any one particular party's "side", but to help mediate these family discussions and decision making.

The discussion must keep the care recipient at the center and avoid other family drama or unresolved issues. If those unrelated issues rear their ugly heads in the discussion, set a separate time to deal with them. The focus of these discussions should be around the care recipient and their best interests. This type of intervention can help alleviate family quarrels. Ultimately the care recipient's values, wishes, and beliefs should always be upheld, and it is the primary caregiver's responsibility to ensure this. This is what makes the earlier section on legal documents so important, because it can avoid many of these problems. You will have a much harder time accomplishing anything else in this book if you don't have the legal foundation first.

For those without family members to share the care responsibilities, the type of unbiased professional advocate we talked about can also provide you with the much-needed support you don't get elsewhere. And, remember the community support network we talked about in an earlier chapter? Your care recipient's circle of friends, organizations that they were actively involved in, and their faith community if they were a part of one are all good resources to tap into. Furthermore, reach out to your own network. If you are a caregiver that is on your own, your support network is even more important. You are likely to be surprised by how many people are able and willing to help in your care recipient's time of need, even if it is just a friendly visit once a week or a meal train to take some of the burden off you and your family.

Another strategy for your burnout-avoidance plan is to routinely carve out time for self-care so that you do not feel like you have lost yourself in caregiving. Don't forget about the importance of filling your own cup so that you are capable of providing the loving support your care recipient needs. A study found that more than 60 percent of caregivers report that their eating habits became worse after beginning to provide informal care to someone and over 50 percent reduced or stopped all exercise. Furthermore, 72 percent reported that they have not attended routine doctor appointments as often as they should since they began providing care.[54] The responsibilities of caregiving undoubtedly account for the neglect in caring for oneself; they may have cut out those self-care activities because they are either too busy with the task of caregiving, or perhaps they can't handle the idea of going to another doctor on their "day off." No matter the reason, they do not prioritize their own care but only that of their care recipient. The neglect of preventative health measures and routine screenings can mean that conditions like breast cancer, for example, are not caught at an early stage when they can be treated. Instead they aren't found until they have progressed and are even life-threatening.

In addition to addressing your own medical care, you will regularly need to just take a break or participate in activities that you enjoy so that you do not feel too overwhelmed. Exercise, read, meditate, stay social, and get adequate sleep. It is important to maintain a balance in your life. A key to employing this

---

[54] Study of Caregivers in Decline Findings from a National Survey September 2006 Evercare in collaboration with National Alliance for Caregiving

strategy is learning to say "no". Caregivers tend to have a hard time doing this. We are givers. We want to help! When I think of most caregivers, I imagine the giving tree in Shel Silverstein's famous poem the Giving Tree. We give and give until there is nothing left but a stump.

When I was running my home care company, I worked with a coach to help me build out processes and employ strategies to scale it. Her name is Crystel Smith, and I had met her when her Grandmother moved into the nursing facility where I worked. She wrote the foreword for this book, describing her own caregiving experience. We remained friends long after our interaction in the nursing facility and at the time I hired her to coach me, I had a big vision for my company. I also had two children under the age of three. One of my biggest challenges was time and balancing priorities. Crystal brought something very insightful to my attention. My schedule was all over the place. There was no consistency, and it was always full of things I was doing for others. Commitments I had made without leaving myself any time for my own business's needs. I was hesitant to ever say no to a request because I never wanted to miss an opportunity or disappoint anyone. However, as Crystal pointed out, every "yes" is a "no" to something else. I was saying yes to everything and as a result saying no to the time I needed to spend on my family, myself, and my business. This is very common in caregivers, and females in particular. Crystel went on to write an excellent book on the subject, which I will reference in the index. What is crucial to remember is that as caregivers, we need to keep our priorities in strict order so that we don't run out of ourselves to give. Furthermore, do not hold back in asking for help when you need it. If caregiving begins to become too overwhelming and you find you cannot balance it with other areas of your life, you may want to consider bringing in some of the outside resources we outlined in this book to help. The next section will outline some ideas for sharing the caregiver burden within a family.

Finally, I encourage you to nurture your relationship with your care recipient. It's easy to get lost in the mundane tasks that you are now taking on for your care recipient. But, make sure you are also taking time to do things together that you both enjoy. Set aside time to enjoy activities together that nurture your relationship and keep you feeling connected to one another in a positive way.

This connection will carry you through the hard times and remind you of why you are doing this. The following section will explore this and other relationships in more detail.

CAREGIVING AND RELATIONSHIPS

It is important to recognize that taking on a caregiving role will inevitably impact your relationships. Starting with the relationship with your care recipient, and trickling into the other relationships in your life. It is crucial to be aware of this and monitor it closely. Of course, every family is different, and each relationship has its own challenges. When your relationship with an aging or disabled family member catapults into the new dynamic of caregiver/care recipient, all bets are off. The core of what your relationship once was, good or bad, is now completely different, and more complicated. If your relationship was weak before, it will certainly be more strained now. It it was strong, it is amazing how easily it can deteriorate. But for some, it can become stronger through the process.

It is important to remember that both you, the caregiver, and the care recipient are in an extremely vulnerable position. You are pouring out so much of yourself to help them on a regular basis. Having another person completely dependent on you is very emotionally, physically, and mentally draining. It is hard to stay positive when you are so exhausted.

Before I became a parent, I never imagined what it would feel like to have another person's life so fully intertwined and dependent on my own. The joys and challenges of parenthood are almost entirely unparalleled in life, but caring for an aging parent can feel very much the same. Parenting and caregiving do share many commonalities. This presents one of what I find to be the most challenging aspects to caring for an aging family member, especially a parent—the resentment that the parent can feel by being "parented" by their child.

Remember, you may feel like you're experiencing a role reversal, but your care recipient is not your child, and they should not be treated as such. It is easy to find oneself in a power struggle of who is parenting whom when it comes to an elder caregiving relationship. I have observed this in both my own family and in my work with caregivers. The caregiver often feels underappreciated or even that the care recipient is unfairly adversarial towards them. Oftentimes, adult children expressed their frustration at how their aging family member would never "listen" to them, but would willingly take the advice of a professional, especially when the professionals are echoing everything that they have suggested.

It is important to remember that care recipients have lost so much, including their sense of independence and autonomy. They are constantly grieving that loss. And while it is not fair and seemingly counter-intuitive, we often take our stress out on those closest to us. Combat this with open communication with your care recipient that is honest, respectful, and includes them in all decision making. Help them maintain as much independence as possible by supporting their decision making and also watching out for their best interests at all times. It is important to recognize that your care recipient has the right to make decisions for themselves, even bad ones. As much as you want to protect them, sometimes supporting them involves allowing them to make choices that you don't agree with and doing what you can to minimize the likelihood of a negative outcome. The caregiver and care recipient alike must be able to recognize the position that the other is in and try to put the shoe on the other foot with every disagreement.

I urge you to be patient with your care recipient during this season of your relationship and remember that your days with them are numbered. The struggles you are having are temporary, and so is this time you have with them. Try to support one another through the difficult times and preserve the value in the relationship you have always had.

MARRIAGE AND CAREGIVING

As a caregiver who is also in a marriage, or any committed relationship, you may have concerns about how your caregiving role will affect this relationship. This is a valid concern. In America, divorce rates have steadily increased since the 1970s. This can be attributed largely to legal changes as well as societal norms, but conflicts in the marriage such as infidelity, financial strain, substance abuse, and irreconcilable differences are also often cited. It makes sense that the strains of elder caregiving could also be damaging to a marriage.

Many caregivers feel they do not receive enough support from their spouse. The spouse often feels neglected, as caregiving is very emotionally taxing, and it can leave you with very little left in the tank to be able to show affection to your significant other. Resentment and loneliness can start to break the relationship down and sometimes the marriage will be unable to survive under the pressures of caregiving.

Gender roles do play a significant factor here. Women are providing an estimated 66 percent of elder care support in the United States.[55] And while men also provide assistance, women may spend as much as 50% more time doing so than men.[56] Unfortunately, this can leave things somewhat unbalanced between genders. In the 1960s, with the feminist movement, many women began to enter the workforce. We have come a long way since then. However, even today, women are still fighting for equal treatment in the workplace. One of the main reasons is the question of whether a female can be as committed as a man to a career while also juggling the responsibilities of child-rearing. In today's world women make up almost half of the United States workforce, and 70 percent of women with children under the age of 18 work outside of the home.[57] This means women are not only participating almost equally as men in the labor force, but they are also still providing an overwhelming majority of the caregiving roles.

In my experience, most but not all of the time it is the daughter, daughter-in-law, or wife of another male relative who takes on the primary responsibility of caregiving. They provide support that is more hands-on in nature, whether that be cleaning, shopping, driving to appointments, filling prescriptions, and even personal or medical care. If the male counterparts are involved, it is most often in a less hands-on supportive role such as managing the finances. I don't point this out to minimize the caregiving efforts of the male gender, but simply to give the most realistic picture of this group's demographics.

---

[55] National Alliance for Caregiving and AARP. (2009). Caregiving in the U.S
[56] https://www.caregiver.org/women-and-caregiving-facts-and-figures
[57] Department of Labor statistics

A marriage is a team, and that team should work together to weather any storm. When times are good, teamwork is easy. There needs to be a commitment from both parties to share in both the burdens and joys of life. When faced with a complex challenge such as caregiving, the relationship needs to be even more of a priority. It will take the coordinated effort of both parties to make the marriage work through the stressors and challenges. This may not come easy, and it needs to be consistently revisited. The key here is the S in the "Guess" acronym- setting boundaries. You must set manageable boundaries with your spouse so that they know what you need during this season in your life. When embarking on the caregiving journey, you must discuss what this will mean for them and your relationship. The expectations must be realistic and the communication clear to avoid misunderstandings. If your partner doesn't support you embarking on this caregiving journey from the beginning, there are going to be unavoidable conflicts along the way. It is much better to be aware of this up front and face it head on than find out in the middle of it.

It is essential to prioritize spending time with your partner, but this cannot be one-sided. You and your partner need to continue to feel valued by one another throughout your caregiving journey. Carve out the time for one another, and it doesn't have to be elaborate date nights. Simply enjoying each other's company, in any setting, can be refreshing for a marriage. Keep it simple, so it doesn't seem like another "chore". Perhaps even prioritizing self care together such as going to the gym or for a long walk. If your caregiving responsibilities are too burdensome to make this happen, you must explore options to alleviate some of that burden as we have discussed in earlier chapters.

The spouse of a caregiver should be understanding, supportive, and kind. Conversely, the caregiving spouse must be careful not to unjustly burden their spouse with their negative emotions and stress by taking it out on them. It is natural for your spouse to be your support system emotionally, but it is also crucial for the supportive spouse of a caregiver to feel appreciated for what they sacrifice during this season. If there is no balance between the two, your supportive spouse is going to get burned out quickly. If you are in either position and do not feel you are getting the support you need from your partner, I would strongly suggest seeking counseling before the damage becomes too severe to repair. Regular counseling is a good practice for couples in any stage or condition of the marriage. It is like regular health maintenance. One should not see a doctor only when sick but routine check ups help us stay tuned in to our bodies, have realistic expectations and know what it takes to maintain our health. The same goes for a marriage. The healthier the foundation, the less likely the marriage will crumble under the strain of caregiving or any other burden.

Finally, if your care recipient IS your spouse, there is a whole other set of dynamics. As a caregiving spouse, you are not only taking on the physical and emotional strain of caring for another person, but you are also grief stricken by losing part or all of the intimacy of your romantic relationship. Earlier we explored the idea of Maslow's hierarchy of needs, and identified the need for love and belonging in relation to socialization. However the need for the romantic or sexual type of intimacy is not spoken about much in terms of caregiving spouses. It is important to remember, you are not losing the intimate relationship but are trading out the intimacy you have known your entire marriage for an entirely different type. The deepening of the connection between caregiving and care receiving spouses can be extremely rewarding. The key is changing your mindset and thinking about intimacy differently. The amount of trust that is necessary to exist between caregiver and care recipient is extremely intimate. It is also important to remember to talk to one another. The mundane tasks of the day to day of caregiving can become so rote that you forget to talk. Sharing your feelings, thoughts, and humor with one another through the daily experiences will go a long way in keeping intimacy alive.

Consider again the "U" in the GUESS acronym- understanding your care recipient. During your marriage, what type of physical connection gave them the most joy? Human touch is key to intimacy. By increasing other types of touch- holding hands, kissing, and embracing for example, you can still enjoy the intimacy that the reduction or absence of sexual intimacy may be negatively affecting. Many married couples no longer sleep together when one becomes more physically debilitated than the other. I advise against this. Of course, you must do what works best for you but I believe that as long as physically possible it is crucial in a marriage to stay connected through shared sleeping arrangements. If sleeping in the same room equates to the caregiving spouse not being able to get adequate sleep, perhaps a respite caregiving arrangement once a week or even every few days will allow for the caregiving spouse to catch up on the needed shut eye to stay refreshed.

PARENTING AND CAREGIVING

I mentioned earlier in the book how I distinctly remember my father's juggling act of parenting and caregiving, and what a demanding and thankless job it is. You are constantly giving 100 percent of yourself to someone else, so how can one possibly do this simultaneously for more than one person? And as average life expectancies increase, the period of time during which one may be caring for both young children and an aging care recipient increases as well. A caregiver may even find themselves in the throes of this juggling act for years or even decades.

One strategy for effective "sandwich caregiving" is to include children in the caregiving process. It is widely recommended by experts in pediatrics that being transparent and open with children about the aging process is best for the mental health of those children and is also generally good for the lessening of stigmas related to aging. Children may ask probing questions that can be uncomfortable at first but speaking directly with children about what is happening with their aging family member will provide reassurance to the child that nothing is "wrong" and that aging is a natural process that should be accepted, not hidden. It can also be quite refreshing to an older adult when a child is forthright with them, doesn't ignore his or her physical challenges but embraces them and seeks to understand. Older adults can often feel ignored or cast aside, so a child's acceptance and curiosity is actually welcomed.

My now six-year-old was scared of his great grandmother the first time we visited her. I count myself lucky to still have great grandparents on both sides of my family for my kids to know. I am going to keep to myself which great-grandmother I am speaking of, because I hope they will both read this book and I would rather they both assume this story is about the other. My son, Cooper, was very shy around his great grandmother on our first visit when he was old enough to interact with her, which I guess was about age 4. He did not say much and stayed on the other side of the room. I encouraged more interaction but he was hesitant. On the ride home, he told me that he was scared of her because of her wrinkles. He said her face was scary and looked like a "halloween mask". This broke my heart. I wanted so badly for my kids to experience the love of their great grandparents since it was something I was never able to enjoy. I took the opportunity to explain to Cooper that his great grandmother's winkles were badges of honor. She has them because she has lived a long time, learned a lot, faced a lot of hurdles, and came through them. She is wrinkly because she is strong. She is wrinkly because she is wise. She is wrinkly because she has lived. She is the farthest thing from scary– she is loving, kind and warm hearted. It took Cooper a while to warm up to this idea but eventually after another visit or two he decided he liked her. I think it may honestly have been the fresh baked cookies that won him over. Either way, he is now very fond of his wrinkly, amazing great grandmother.

Children of any age can take part in the caregiving process at various levels. Simply taking your child along for visits and including them in the conversations is a good place to start. Children are often "sheltered" from the aging process, but, exposing your young children to aging is effective in preparing them to understand and more easily accept their own aging and mortality. By the time a child reaches adolescence, finding a common ground with their elder family members can be much more challenging. Teenagers tend to be self-absorbed and can be harder for older adults to relate to. So, starting young is a much easier approach. If you do not have an aging family member for them to interact with at a young age, you can also introduce them to the elder generation by volunteering at a local senior living community. Senior living communities can always use an extra set of hands!

There are numerous benefits to intergenerational contact for both the adult and the child. We touched on this subject in an earlier chapter. The benefits for the older adult may be more obvious, such as reducing social isolation and depression, but there are numerous benefits for the child as well. Some examples are:

· Dispelling irrational fears or beliefs that children may have of elders and aging (such as "wrinkles" are scary)

· Storytelling—passing down family values and history

· Giving the child a sense of purpose

· Giving the child an opportunity to learn a new skill from the older adult

· Pride in their background/family roots

Another challenge sandwich caregivers face is balancing the duties and responsibilities of the caregiving role so that they do not take away from those of the parenting role. Everyone in the family unit must be flexible and understanding with one another, but children do need to know that while the family commitment of caregiving is important, the commitment to their well-being and development is equally so. If their caregiving parent never makes it to their dance recital or soccer game because of their caregiving responsibilities, they will feel less valued as a part of the family unit.

I recommend using a calendar tool (either a literal paper calendar to hang on a wall in a shared space or an online calendar that the entire family has access to), and allowing each family member to put activities that are important to them on the schedule. Using a different color for each family member's activities can provide a visual representation of the percentage of time being spent on what each family member feels is important and help everyone be more willing to compromise and adjust accordingly when needed.

It is important to remember that your children are watching and learning from you all the time. They are like sponges- they pick up on everything, both verbal and non verbal. The example you set with your approach to caregiving and the boundaries you implement will carry with them into adulthood and potentially their own caregiving journeys one day.

CAREGIVING AND WORK

Arguably one of the most challenging aspects of being a caregiver, particularly for the sandwich generation, is balancing work and caregiving. While this might not be the first "relationship" that comes to mind when you embark on your caregiving journey, as your care recipient becomes increasingly dependent on you, the relationship with your employer may become strained. According to the

National Alliance for Caregiving, six out of ten caregivers also report working, and 61 percent report experiencing at least one work-related impact.[58]

The modern workforce has not caught up to the idea that families no longer can afford to have one "breadwinner" that supports the family financially while the other manages the home and family needs. Therefore, many families depend on the dual income of two working adults, and insurance is a vital benefit often being provided through the employer. Not to mention that caregiving can also add financial burden to the household. And did I mention single parents?

For some, it may seem as if quitting your job or cutting back your hours is the only option. However, for many people this is simply not an option. Leaving the workforce at prime working age, even temporarily, can also have devastating effects on one's career. You could potentially be giving up opportunities for advancement, lowering overall income potential, missing out on retirement investment matching and reducing future Social Security benefits. It is a struggle akin to a parent taking time off to stay at home with babies and young children. And for those with lower income, the choice is often made because if they did work, all or most of the income would go towards paying for daycare.

The sad reality is, we have a long way to go as a society in supporting family caregivers. There are, however, some ways you can set yourself up for success by being prepared to advocate for yourself in the workplace. First and foremost, it is very important to know your rights. You may qualify for the protections of the Family Medical Leave Act, which offers job protection to employees who have a family member with a "serious health condition" to take unpaid leave (up to 12 weeks annually). Upon return from this leave, the employee must be permitted to return to the same job or one that is equivalent in pay, benefits, terms and conditions. It also guarantees their group health benefits will be maintained during the leave.[59]

To qualify for FMLA leave you must have worked for an employer for at least 20 work weeks during the past 12 months. FMLA applies to all public and private sector employers of 50 or more employees. Unfortunately, not many people can

[58] CAREGIVING IN THE U.S. 2020: EXECUTIVE SUMMARY
[59] dol.gov/agencies/whd/fmla

afford to take 12 weeks unpaid, and another challenge with it is the required 30-day notice in advance of taking the leave, meaning that unexpected health emergencies may not be covered.[60]

In 2018, the United States Congress passed the RAISE Act (Recognize, Assist, Include, Support and Engage).[61] This law requires the Department of Health and Human Services to develop a council which will make recommendations on more effective models of support for family caregivers and strategies to improve federal support of programs related to family caregiving. While the council has yet to put forth any concrete recommendations, their priorities do include workplace policies to better enable family caregivers to keep working, which is indicative of positive changes to come.

In addition to knowing the laws and your rights as an employee, a key strategy you can adopt on your own is opening a dialogue before your employer takes notice or hears of your caregiving journey from another employee. You might be currently hiding your caregiving role and its associated struggles from your employer, but it is important to have an open discussion with your supervisor to let them know about the family challenges you are facing. They may be willing to adjust your work schedule, offer flex time, job sharing or temporary telecommuting. Some employers may also offer caregiving benefits above and beyond FMLA. For instance, as of October 2016 a little over half of US employers offered some type of "Employee Assistance Programs".[62] Check with your company's HR Director to determine what benefits might be offered by your employer.

Whether additional benefits are available or not, the more your employer knows about your caregiving needs, the easier they can accommodate you. However, be sure to remain as flexible and accommodating from your end as possible, so that your supervisor can see that you are committed to your job and desire to keep from burdening others in the workplace. Once you and your supervisor have come up with an agreed-upon plan, particularly if special accommodations are being made for you to better balance your work

---

[60] dol.gov/agencies/whd/fmla
[61] caregiving.org/advocacy/raise-family-caregivers-act/
[62] U.S. Department of Labor statistics

and caregiving responsibilities, be sure to follow up with an acknowledgment of the plan in writing. In this correspondence once again emphasize your commitment to your job and appreciation for the accommodations. This will not only make your supervisor feel good about supporting you, but it gives you clear documentation of what has been agreed upon should any questions come up later. Any time anything changes on your end, or either side deviates from the plan, be sure to also document that as well.

If you have tried this approach already and you feel you are being unfairly treated by your employer due to your caregiving responsibilities, you may be subject to discrimination under state or federal law. There are several federal and state laws that prohibit this type of discrimination, and each year in the U.S., the number of cases reported to the Equal Employment Opportunity Commission is growing rapidly. It may benefit you to speak to an EEOC attorney about your individual situation to receive added guidance.

Finally, keep in mind that the likelihood of an epic work/life balance tug of war is high. So how does the caregiver who needs to work manage this situation? The primary solutions are good planning, preparation and communication. Too many people avoid the issue until it becomes a crisis, which ends up being most problematic for you, your care recipient, and your employer. Overnight the situation can go from bad to worse, such as in the event of a fall or other life altering incident that seriously inhibits your care recipient's independence. Without a good plan in place, something like this can throw everything spiraling into chaos, and once it begins it is very hard to regain control. Plan ahead and don't let yourself fall victim to this costly scenario. Also, remember that bringing in an aging life care manager can help you navigate the complexities of the senior care world, and support you by stepping in when you can't take your attention away from work or other responsibilities.

CAREGIVERS HAVE FEELINGS, TOO

Now, let's talk about a subject that rarely gets attention in the world of caregiving – the emotional turmoil that can come along with the role. Caregivers may feel an array of emotions throughout their journey and the various ups and downs. These emotional surges are normal. However, some of the emotions that can arise when undertaking a caregiving role can be extremely difficult and even surprising when they rear their ugly heads. It is easy to be taken off guard and completely thrown for a loop. Therefore, at each stage of your caregiving journe, you will need to ensure you are recognizing your feelings, working through them, and taking good care of yourself.

This section covers a subject that rarely gets attention in the world of caregiving – the emotional turmoil that can come along with the role. Caregivers may feel an array of emotions throughout the various ups and downs of their journey. Some of the emotions that can arise can even be surprising when they rear their ugly heads. It can be like a roller coaster at times. It is easy to be taken off guard and completely thrown for a loop.

Please recognize that these emotional surges are normal, and it is imperative as a caregiver to acknowledge and process your feelings. At each stage of your caregiving journey, make sure you are recognizing your feelings, working through them, and taking good care of yourself. I implore you, do not be afraid to engage in counseling or therapy to work through your feelings about being a caregiver.

Furthermore, caregiving can be very isolating. Individuals who you thought were your friends may be there in the short term but those relationships may falter over time. We talked at length about how dangerous isolation can be for older adults earlier in this book. The same goes for caregivers! Support groups for caregivers allow for the members to express their concerns and fears without concern about judgment, which can help reduce stress.

Some of the most difficult feelings to manage may include guilt, resentment, anxiety, anger, fear, frustration and even grief. Let's explore some of the emotions caregivers commonly experience.

GUILT

One of the most common emotions I have heard expressed by caregivers is guilt. Guilt can be caused by a gamut of reasons. You may find yourself feeling that you are not giving enough to your care recipient. Guilt can also be the byproduct of feeling other negative emotions and then regretting feeling that way. You may feel guilty about your relationship with your care recipient deteriorating, particularly if it was a close personal relationship prior. If your care recipient gets ill or injured, you may feel guilty that you did not do enough to prevent it.

One of the primary causes of guilt is "broken" promises. I touched on this before, in relation to the common promise of keeping a care recipient at home and avoiding the nursing home. The guilt arises when that promise isn't practical to keep. Sometimes senior living placement is the safest option for an elderly adult, and you may be facing the guilt that sets in when you are forced to choose between their safety and your loyalty. If this is you, I understand and respect how you feel. There is no reason to feel guilty about prioritizing safety and well-being. And as we discussed in an earlier chapter, the reality is that there are a variety of choices of lifestyle in senior community living today that are nothing like "nursing homes" of the past so the perception of "nursing home" that your care recipient had in mind when they asked you to honor their wish is probably cliché and/or outdated. You can counterbalance your guilt by making an educated choice that you can feel good about, knowing that your care recipient is going to receive high quality care in a comfortable and safe environment.

As I mentioned, guilt can also come from feeling like we are not giving enough of ourselves to our caregiving role. Frequently caregivers will recognize their need for a break, but then feel guilty when they call upon their support system to step in. But if every minute they spend separate from their care recipient is guilt ridden, are they really getting the break they need? To address this, I must return to the topic of caregiver burnout. To be the best caregiver you can be does not mean to do every single task yourself.

Regardless of the source, the feeling of guilt in caregiving is a common theme, and you are not likely to avoid it completely. Because of the commonality amongst caregivers, support groups are particularly helpful in sharing and overcoming feelings of guilt. There are a multitude of different types of support groups, there is one for virtually every type of condition or situation. Some are facilitated by professionals and some are member-led. Of course, each group is unique in its dynamics and how it operates. You may not find the right fit easily or right away. To help you hone in on the right one for you, I have put together a guide on this subject for this chapter.

RESENTMENT

Resentment can exist in a caregiver/care recipient relationship for many reasons, and it is a two-way street. Neither caregiver nor care recipient has chosen to be in this position. So by being put in a situation by force, feelings of resentment are normal. It is important to recognize that you resent the situation, not the person.

It is human nature to desire independence. Therefore, most care recipients feel resentful of being fully reliant on another person. Accepting help is difficult to do, and can cause a lot of negative emotions. This is often the reason care recipients take their resentful feelings out on their caregivers. As caregivers, it is easy to feel unappreciated and even hurt by our care recipient's words and actions when they are expressing these feelings. Recognizing and acknowledging that your care recipient does not mean to hurt you, but they are hurting themselves, is a helpful first step. Next, consider telling your care recipient how you feel. Most likely, they do not want to damage the relationship and will try to express their emotions in a healthier way.

Old tensions from the past may also rear their ugly head when you are thrust into a caregiving situation. Relationships are messy, and oftentimes unresolved conflicts from the past remain in the background even when the care recipient's physical needs are in the forefront. This is something that during my career I have always made a point to keep in the back of my mind. When an older adult needs care, it is the adult child that the medical and care community assumes is going to step up and provide that care. When adult children seem aloof, uncaring or even disdainful, it is easy to judge them. However, we as professionals do not know their history or the details of their past relationship.

When I worked at a law firm we had a client, Nathan, whose mother was in a nursing facility after her spouse had passed. He had not spoken to his abusive mother in over 20 years. She had walked out of his life entirely. The nursing home social worker tracked him down and asked him to step in to handle his mother's affairs. Without his intervention, his mother would have become a ward of the state. He decided to graciously accept the responsibility and contacted us for guidance on what to do. I was truly humbled by the experience of watching him step into his mother's life as an advocate and caregiver when she needed him most, even when she had not done the same for him as a child. This may have been the best way for him to resolve some of the painful past.

I realize what Nathan did is hard. You may not be able to step into this role at all, and that is ok. There is no wrong answer here. If you decide it is better for you to remain at a distance for your own mental health, then you should do just that. If you find it is hard to remain a positive advocate for your care recipient because of buried negative feelings, then you may not be the best suited person for the role. You can set up an advocacy team and then step out. You can even hire a professional guardian for your care recipient so that you don't have to make medical and care decisions. This may be what is best for both you and them. However, before making that decision consider that stepping into this role can be very rewarding even for a strained or non-existent relationship and do not make the decision lightly. Speak with your support system or your therapist about it and consider carefully. Then, move forward with peace and confidence in your decision.

Finally, if you are the primary caregiver, resentment may also brew between you and siblings or others in your family who do not step up to help. We addressed this topic previously and I suggested the family meeting and provided a checklist to help structure it. But, if you find this does not work with your family, it is likely to be more frustrating to you to continue trying to insist that non-interested family members help you, so don't try to force it. Accept that you are in an unbalanced situation and move on, seeking your support from other sources. Trust me when I tell you that you will sleep better at night than those who are not doing their fair share.

FRUSTRATION

At any point in your caregiving journey have you ever felt like you were just going to "snap"? Frustration such as this is another very common feeling caregivers experience. I think frustration sums up a lot of the aforenamed feelings into one, and it can be hard at times to even pinpoint why you are frustrated; you just find yourself "one edge". You might have a feeling that no matter what you do, your care recipient isn't going to get better or be happy. As I mentioned, many care recipients resent being so dependent on another person. Frequently, they end up taking their frustration out on those who do the most for them, even when inside they are truly grateful. This in turn is very frustrating for caregivers.

If left unchecked, frustration may lead to serious problems. Don't be afraid to "let it out", but do so in a safe way. For example, scream in an empty room. Watch a sad movie and let yourself have a good cry. Let it out once in a while when it seems overwhelming and seek healthy ways to relieve your frustration on a regular basis such as exercise and routine self care.

ANXIETY

If you didn't have a family, a spouse, a job, or any other responsibilities, what a superhero caregiver you could be! But, guess what?! You do have other responsibilities. Many caregivers are perfectionists. If you are prone to perfectionist tendencies pre-caregiving, it is only natural to expect them to be heightened once you are in this role. In fact, perfectionists in a family are more likely to volunteer for caregiving roles because they believe they can do it best. This tends to apply in greater numbers to women than men. Furthermore, since many more women are caregivers than men, and women are more prone to anxiety than men- perhaps up to twice as much, it follows logically that anxiety is rampant amongst caregivers.

The unrealistic expectations we place on ourselves do nothing but cause us unwarranted anxiety. Heed my warning that perfectionism as a caregiver is the ultimate cause of anxiety and in turn, caregiver burnout. This is because you are answering to the toughest critic you have ever had – yourself. To combat this, consider what your triggers are and remain vigilant for them. The root of perfectionism usually stems from comparison. You may begin comparing yourself to others and feeling "less than". You may even be comparing yourself to another version of yourself, the caregiver that you wish you could be. But, your care recipient doesn't need another version of you. They need you. They need your compassion. They need trust. They need you to care. They do not need you to be perfect.

To set yourself up for success, you must accept that there is no such thing as the perfect caregiver, and focus on your strengths, while finding opportunities to lean on supports in areas you identify as weaknesses. Furthermore, focus only on what you can control at this current time. Do not let the "what ifs" and "if onlys" consume you. Take it one day at a time, and don't forget to celebrate the small wins as they come(such as, mom took a shower today!).

ANGER

Anger is another extremely common emotion for caregivers to experience. Experiencing anger may then cause you to be fearful. You may become scared because you cannot recognize where the anger came from or how to control it. As I mentioned, some emotions on this journey may surprise you. But remember that you will experience these natural human emotions and it does not mean that you are incapable of caring for your care recipient. The key is dealing with the anger in a healthy way.

Anger can affect both men and women, but it may manifest itself more in male caregivers than their female counterparts. Men are much more likely than women to let their emotions fester under the surface and they can boil over into angry outbursts if not dealt with. Sometimes anger is what we see on the outside, but there is a deeper underlying emotion inside that is manifesting itself as anger.

It can be helpful to try and identify what triggers your anger. Once you know what a trigger is, you can be more prepared when it happens and therefore avoid or at least reduce episodes of anger. The truth is, anger could be coming from any number of different places. That is something you will want to address is therapy and begin to work through with a professional.

In the moment, it is important to recognize that you are not angry at your care recipient. Even if it may feel that way, you do not want to misplace your anger. You may be angry at the situation, the disease they have, or the circumstances. If you have identified anger as an emotion you are struggling with, it is crucial to address it professionally. If it remains out of control, it can lead to unintended episodes of abuse. It is not possible for anyone to be in complete control of their emotions all the time. If you get angry and say or do something you don't mean, be kind to yourself. There is grace to start new tomorrow. But, you must recognize the warning signs and take steps to get it under control.

FEAR

Fear and anxiety are closely linked. Fear is related to your feelings about the future. Dreading what may happen if you are not in control makes you fearful of what lies ahead. You may be worried that you will forget or miss something that will have catastrophic results, and therefore are constantly worrying. If you are not a trained caregiver, you may also be afraid that you will misstep. That you will do something wrong.

Fear can cripple us. Therefore, we cannot ignore it. We must face it head on. The best way to do this is to take its power away. We have to live in the moment. Do not worry about what the future holds. Focus on what you can do today, and let go of trying to anticipate what will come next. My father in law is known for saying "do something, even if it's wrong". I love this because we so often let fear stop us from taking a step forward. When in reality, the step forward, even if it is unsteady, is getting us closer to where we need to be. You will make mistakes. That is okay, you are human. The key is learning from the mistakes and not letting fear keep up from moving forward.

Being well prepared can also help with alleviating fear. Caregivers who are ill prepared experience more fear because fear of the unknown is scarier than fear of what we do know. Therefore, putting together a good caregiving plan and support system can go a long way in diminishing fear.

GRIEF

Caregivers often begin to experience grief long before their care recipient passes. As your care recipient loses their physical and mental abilities, you may grieve not being able to connect with them in the ways that you used to. Their personality may change drastically, especially with a cognitive illness like dementia, and the person you care about and enjoyed being with seems to be already gone.

It is important to remember to nurture your relationship. It's easy to get lost in the mundane tasks that you are now taking on for them. But, make sure you are also taking time to do things together that you both enjoy. Set aside time to enjoy activities together that nurture your relationship and keep you feeling connected to them in a positive way.

Furthermore, there are other losses that caregivers may be grieving while caring for their care recipient. Perhaps other relationships suffer, friendships may be lost, you may have lost the ability to continue doing work that you love or hobbies you enjoy. There is a loss of your own freedom and independence as a caregiver when someone is so fully reliant on you.

And then, when your care recipient does pass on, the roller coaster of emotions doesn't end. With the passing of someone you have been caring for, there comes a natural grief but also in many cases a sense of relief. This sense of relief can bring us back to the feelings of guilt. It is a vicious cycle. Grief is not linear. It is a process that encompasses many different emotions that can come in waves. It cannot be summed up in one particular feeling or experience, and everyone grieves differently.

One resource that is frequently underutilized is the bereavement services of Hospice. We talked about the immense support Hospice can provide while your care recipient is in their end of life stage. But a lesser known benefit is the support for the bereaved after the patient has passed. Let me repeat: Grief is not linear. You may experience surges of Grief long after your care recipient has passed. Hospice provides counseling services for families of their deceased patients through the process for up to a year after the patient's passing. Support groups you can get plugged into through Hospice may continue on well beyond that. They also provide spiritual support. The type and duration of the services does vary from hospice to hospice, state to state. Local to where I live and work there are hospice companies that even provide these services to people who did not have a care recipient or loved one enrolled in hospital services with their company. They simply provide the service free of charge to anyone in the community who is grieving.

For many it isn't only grief over the loss of the person themselves but also the role that has become such a huge part of their life. Being a caregiver becomes a part of your identity, one that can be hard to let go. If you find you feel this way after you have grieved the loss of your care recipient, you may want to consider doing something that helps fill that void. Perhaps you may consider caregiving as a new career. Or you may try volunteering with a nonprofit organization that works with seniors or the disabled. Perhaps your faith organization could use help with friendly visits to the homebound church congregation members. There are a lot of options and any of them you may find fulfilling.

SUPPORT GROUPS

There are many types of support groups. This guide will help you find the right one for you.*

- **Disease specific:** If your care recipient has a chronic illness or diagnosis, you could turn to the local foundation chapter for the disease for support groups in your area (for example, the Alzheimer's Association)
- **Senior Living Communities:** Oftentimes families of residents in the same senior living community will ban together and create support groups (ask the activities coordinator or resident council president at the community where your care recipient lives)
- Check with your local Department of Veterans Affairs for support groups for **military veterans and their families**
- **Grief:** Your local Hospice company is a good resource for grief support groups
- **Faith based:** check with your church or place of worship for support groups based on your faith
- **Online/virtual:** An online or social media support group can be more flexible for working caregivers
  - › On Facebook there are the Caregivers Hub, Caregivers Connect and Memory People
- **Adult Children of Aging Parents:** This organization is still relatively in its infancy but growing fast – acapcommnity.org
- **Death Cafes:** open honest discussion about death and dying– deathcafe.com
- **Book clubs:** if the structure of a support group is not favorable for you, try a book club instead as you may still find support and community that you are looking for without feeling intimidated

If you can't find one you like that fits your schedule, consider starting your own. The chances are someone else is out there looking for the same thing and not finding it. So, blaze the trail! Place an announcement in the paper or do a social media post to make others aware of what you are doing and get started.

NOTES

CHAPTER 7

"The simple act of caring is heroic."

-Edward Albert

My final statements come from a place of appreciation and encouragement. As with every family I have had the pleasure to work with, I am truly honored to be a part of your caregiving journey. I am immensely proud of you for taking this step. I understand that taking the time to educate yourself isn't easy, but just like any other challenge you face in your life, the more you know the better the result you will have. The caregiving race is a marathon, not a sprint. It is important to pace yourself and stay in tune with yourself.

At risk of sounding like a broken record, my number one piece of advice for you as you embark on your caregiving journey is to take a preventative approach. Good planning is everything. There are many uncontrollable aspects involved. Without a good plan in place, even a tiny hiccup can throw everything drastically off course.

You can do this most effectively by staying centered on my top five tips for caregivers which are integral pieces of an effective strategy. Here they are again as a refresher:

- Get organized.
- Understand your care recipient.
- Educate yourself.
- Set boundaries.
- Seek Support.

Also remember to be flexible with the plan. Things will not always go according to the plan, and you cannot possibly anticipate all scenarios. With a solid strategy in place and resources at your fingertips, course-correcting goes so much smoother. As you travel this journey, remain open minded and consider all options so you don't box yourself in. You may not need all of the information and advice outlined in this book, and some of the areas I only touched on you will need much more. There are many books on these varying topics that I would suggest adding to your toolbox. Please be sure to reference the list I have put together in the index. Please use this book as a tool to guide you throughout your journey.

I will warn you that you will receive a lot of advice along the way. I say "warn" because while advice can be helpful, it can also be hurtful. While it is always a good idea to ask for advice and seek support from others who have walked this path, do not assume your caregiving journey will or should look like anyone else's. This is a dangerous assumption that will only lead to frustration on your part. Remember to do what is best for your family and situation, and do not compare yourself to others.

Based on the fact that you are reading this book I know you take this responsibility seriously and care tremendously. You are a caregiver, but you are not JUST a caregiver. Don't let your self-identity be reduced to the mundane. Being a caregiver is an extremely honorable thing. There is no shame in it. Wear your badge proudly.

Remember that this is a season. You have no way of knowing how long you will be walking this journey but one day you will look back on it and it will seem much shorter than it was when you were walking it. As a new mom, someone said to me at my baby shower that the days are long but the years are short. I have come to realize how true that statement is and it applies to every aspect of life. There are few experiences in life as simultaneously challenging and rewarding as caregiving. Don't focus on the mountain ridges ahead. Keep your eyes on the path in front of you, and don't forget to take the time to enjoy the little things. And finally, don't be afraid to share with others what you are going through. Hearing your story may be exactly what they need at a difficult point in their journey. Take heart in knowing that you are NOT alone, we are all in this together.

NOTES

NOTES

LIST OF RECOMMENDED BOOKS

General Aging/Caregiving:

This Chair Rocks by Ashton Applewhite

A Bittersweet Season by Jane Gross

The Empowered Caregiver: Practical Advice and Emotional Support for Adult Children of Aging Parents by Linda Fodrini-Johnson

What Are Old People For?: How Elders Will Save the World by William H. Thomas

From a Christian Perspective:

As My Parents Age by Cynthia Ruchti

Caring for our Aging Parents: Lessons in Love, Loss, and Letting Go by Michele Howe

Alzheimer's and Dementia:

The 36-Hour Day by Nancy L. Mace and Peter V. Rabins

Learning to Speak Alzheimer's by Joanne Koenig-Coste

Alzheimer's Through the Stages by Mary Moller

Being My Mom's Mom by Loretta Anne Woodward Veney

Creating Moments of Joy Along the Alzheimer's Journey: A Guide for Families and Caregivers by Jolene Brackey

Brain Health Age You Age by Mansbach, Lyons, Simmons (Prevention focused)

Death and Dying:

Gone from My Sight by Barbara Karnes

Hard Choices for Loving People by Hank Dunn

Being Mortal: Medicine and What Matters in the End by Atul Gawande

Fearless: Facing the Future Confidently with Relational Estate Planning by Joshua E. Hummer, Esq. and Anna Wishart

What Grieving People Wish You Knew by Nancy Guthrie

Caring for the Caregiver:

The Power of No for Women by Crystal Lynn Smith

The Conscious Caregiver: A Mindful Approach to Caring for Your Loved One Without Losing Yourself by Linda Abbit

Dancing with Elephants by Jarem Sawatsky

CREDITS AND ACKNOWLEDGEMENTS

My Editors: Kara Rodriguez and Sherrie Irvin. Thank you both for your generosity with your time and expertise!

My Designer: Hillary Davis. Thank you for bringing my vision to life so perfectly!

My supporters:

Crystel Smith - You and your sweet grandmother were one of the first of many beautiful caregiving stories I have been privileged to witness firsthand. The idea to write this book came from you. Not only are you an inspirational caregiver, but watching you launch your writing career gave me the courage and inspiration to follow my own dream. Thank you for forging the path!

Josh Hummer ("Hummer") - I may never have finished this project if it weren't for your constant support and belief in me. And, for encouraging me to "slow down" this year, I found not only the time but also the perspective I needed to finally get it over the finish line. For that and so many things I will always be grateful to you my friend.

Elizabeth Skordinski - You have been one of my biggest cheerleaders along the way. I am blown away by your support. Thank you for being my "Proverbs 31 woman" role model my dear friend!

Noelia Navarro - Mi amiga, ¿qué puedo decir? You were there with me through a lot of the stories in this book. Thank you for caring for our clients like your own family. Thank you for being my friend and supporter. Estoy agradecido por ti mi amiga de mi alma!

Anna Wishart - When book writing got hard, having you to commiserate with me, and then push me to keep going, was just what I needed. Thank you my "twinsie"!

Laura Smothers-Chu - Your story and path have been so inspirational to me. Thank you for being a shining example of how to care with joy and compassion!

Janet Southward- You reminded me again and again how the world needs this book. Thank you for your constant encouragement!

My husband, Josh- You were the first person I let read this book all the way through and I was terrified to receive your feedback- more than anyone I wanted your approval of my writing. When you said "it's good", I was so relieved and overjoyed! You have always supported me and never let me doubt myself, in this or anything else. You are my rock, my best friend, my partner. I love you.

About the Author:

Pam Reynolds is a passionate advocate for older adults. She experienced the trying difficulties of family caregiving for her ailing grandmother as a teenager. Inspired by this, at a very young age Pam felt a strong pull to make a difference in the lives of older adults and their caregivers. She dedicated herself to this cause by working and educating herself in the field of elder care. She is a Certified Aging Life Care Manager, Certified Professional Gerontologist, and Certified Dementia Practitioner. She has a diverse vocational background that includes assisted living facility and nursing home management, as well as owning a company that helped people age in place at home.

Finding herself frequently meeting with families in crisis is what gave her the idea to write this book. After selling her home care company in 2019, her passion for helping older adults and their caregivers led her into the estate planning and elder law field. There she encountered even more people who had fallen victim to the common pitfalls associated with aging. Even more frustrating for her was to know that in many cases, the crises could have easily been avoided with proper education and preparation. Considering this, Pam knew this book could wait no longer!

Originally from the Winchester Virginia area, Pam now lives in Ashburn Virginia with her husband Josh, who runs a local Civil Engineering office, and her two rambunctious boys, Cooper (age 6) and Corbin (age 5). They keep her running between brazilian jiu-jitsu (Pam is also a student), taekwondo, swimming, church activities and more- there is never a dull moment!

www.ingramcontent.com/pod-product-compliance
Lightning Source LLC
Chambersburg PA
CBHW062050270326
41931CB00013B/3012